Praise

'Unlike the grind of most business books, this is an easy read! It is informative and well-structured with practical takeaways I could implement right away.'
 — **Louise Gardner,** Managing Director, Pledge Consulting

'As a certified behavioural consultant, I highly recommend this power-packed book for all innovative business owners and leaders. Gain the upper hand with top talent in a highly competitive market with this practical and effective people "toolbox".'
 — **Jackie Le Roux,** Founder, Empower Opportunity

'A must-read for any small- to medium-sized business serious about improving company culture and taking the business and its people to the next level.'
 — **Phoebe Brisbane,** Marketing Manager, Strata One

'With practical examples and frameworks, this is a great read for any business owner.'
 — **Lachy Gray,** Co-Founder, Yarno

'The workplace and employees are in a new paradigm and this book has a great balance of why I should read this, what I need to do and how I can do it. I recommend it to any business owner who wants to lead business growth by and through people power!'

— **Sandy Ferguson,** Human Resources Professional

Great People Great Business

Your HR handbook for creating a business that's ready to scale and grow

KAREN KIRTON

Re^think

First published in Great Britain in 2022 by Rethink Press (www.rethinkpress.com)

© Copyright Karen Kirton

All rights reserved. No part of this publication may be reproduced, stored in or introduced into a retrieval system, or transmitted, in any form, or by any means (electronic, mechanical, photocopying, recording or otherwise) without the prior written permission of the publisher.

The right of Karen Kirton to be identified as the author of this work has been asserted by her in accordance with the Copyright, Designs and Patents Act 1988.

This book is sold subject to the condition that it shall not, by way of trade or otherwise, be lent, resold, hired out, or otherwise circulated without the publisher's prior consent in any form of binding or cover other than that in which it is published and without a similar condition including this condition being imposed on the subsequent purchaser.

This book is dedicated to my best friend and husband, Rob, who didn't think I was at all mad to be writing a book and supported me throughout, as he always has.

Contents

Introduction	1
PART ONE Deciding To Create A Great Place To Work	**9**
1 External Drivers	11
The future of work	12
Disruption and transformation	17
Summary	23
2 Internal Drivers	25
Stuck in the day-to-day	26
Employee turnover	28
Compliance	32
Employment policies	36
Summary	39
PART TWO Building A Great Place To Work	**41**
3 Find	43
Your goal culture	44

Setting the structure	49
Recruiting great people	57
Interviewing process	71
Onboarding for success	75
Summary	82
4 Grow	**83**
Growth and development	84
Leadership today	94
Managing performance	104
Communicate, communicate, communicate	116
Summary	128
5 Keep	**131**
Listening	132
Career paths	142
Recognition	146
Rewards	154
Summary	164

PART THREE Maintaining A Great Place To Work 165

6 Measuring	**167**
Measures of success	167
Accountability	174
Summary	180

7 Momentum	**181**
Feedback loops	182
Future focused	184
Summary	189
Conclusion	**191**
References	**195**
Acknowledgements	**205**
The Author	**207**

Introduction

For many successful business owners, the story goes something like this...

Starting with a great idea, you form a new business and, before you realise, you discover that your small business is not so small anymore. You have somewhere between 10 and 100 employees and things become more complex.

When you first started your business, I imagine you thought about finance, cash flow, technology, marketing and sales. Perhaps you assumed that when you needed more people with the right skills, you'd be able to recruit them, and if you paid them well and looked after them, they would stay.

Like many business owners, you've probably since discovered that it's not quite that easy. As you want to scale up and grow your businesses, you are heavily reliant on finding, growing and keeping great people, which can be difficult in a small business environment competing with bigger corporations. If this resonates with you, the good news is that you're not alone. This book can help.

I've worked in Human Resources (HR) for over twenty years, but that wasn't always the case. I have dabbled in sales, customer service and even debt collection. It wasn't until I worked in an organisation that had great HR and I got to see behind the curtain that I understood the impact HR could have on how a business runs and performs. It was then that I decided to study for a Bachelor of Business majoring in HR and Marketing, and later a graduate diploma of psychology. I believe there is incredible power in creating a great place to work, not just for the individual employees, but for your business and the communities it serves.

My first HR role was in a business without a previous HR department, so I was fortunate to be in a situation where the HR team was building the processes and being innovative with the programs. This led to an award in 2005 for the Best HR Team, and in 2006, we won the Best Employer Brand at the Australian HR Awards. It was that experience that gave me, although

INTRODUCTION

I didn't realise it at the time, a unique insight into how to build an HR function. This was a skill I then took to other roles as I became a specialist in creating HR functions and teams.

I worked with different Australian and multinational companies before founding Amplify HR in 2016 as a consulting business to help small and medium-sized enterprises (SMEs) scale up and grow through creating a great place to work.

It is through these experiences that I created the Find, Grow, Keep methodology outlined in this book. It is specifically designed for businesses of fewer than 100 employees to create a workplace which attracts and retains great people.

Many business owners tell me that people are their greatest asset, but they're also their biggest headache. Businesses looking to scale up and grow need great people. Paradoxically, the more people a business has, the more complex and time consuming it becomes for the owner. This slows their ability to grow and thrive.

It is not surprising when you consider how the world and workplaces have changed over time, and continue to do so at a rapid pace. This is why as a business owner, you're in a unique and exciting position, but you may also be exhausted and concerned about the future.

I have found that owners of SMEs believe they need to wait until they are 'large enough' to warrant hiring an internal HR manager. Until then, the founder/owner does what they can to create a nice workplace and hopes it is enough. As one owner told me recently after almost twenty years in business: 'I completely underestimated the value of structured people practices.'

Instead, this business owner had turned to a range of DIY options including leadership courses, implementing HR software, HR call centres, relying on their accountant, recruitment agencies, short-term consultants, virtual assistants, subcontractors, team building/training and sometimes just delegating responsibility to the chief finance officer (CFO) or office manager. Although all these roles and resources can be useful and valuable in certain situations, when your people practices are not structured or part of an overarching program, you end up working on the symptoms, not the reasons for the pain. Ultimately, the headaches remain.

Those who are only interested in the compliance aspects of HR and being reactive with people practices tend to discover that this does not lead to a sustainable business. When they focus on doing the minimum, treating employees as just another business resource, they don't create a workplace that enables employees to do their best and find they are continually fighting fires.

INTRODUCTION

Having worked with such business owners across different industries, I regularly hear these statements:

- 'Why doesn't <name> just do their job?'
- 'I was totally blindsided by <name> leaving.'
- 'I'm stuck in back-to-back meetings and don't have time to even think about the future.'
- 'We just can't seem to get this project off the ground.'
- 'I'm caught in this spiral of hiring and training.'
- 'We're losing some big clients; we need to work on our customer experience (CX) scores.'
- 'I have to work every weekend, otherwise things don't get done.'

If any of this sounds familiar, the Find, Grow, Keep methodology outlined within this book will help. Using real-world examples of businesses I have worked with, I will take you step-by-step through this framework to create a great place to work so your business can scale up and grow.

Research consistently shows that if you can develop a workplace culture that engages your teams, you will enjoy higher customer satisfaction, loyalty, productivity and profitability, and lower employee turnover. You will be able to:

- **Find** great people. As a small business owner, you may find it difficult to attract candidates as you feel you can't compete with what larger corporates have to offer. By creating a compelling employment offer and employer brand, you will be able not only to sell your business more effectively, but to attract candidates who will ask to work for you even when you aren't advertising. Being able to recruit great people not only increases productivity and reduces costs, it also attracts and retains other great people.

- **Grow** great people. Personal development is consistently shown to rate as a top benefit for employees[1] and a reason why they stay longer in a role,[2] but it is often overlooked by businesses. Many SME owners provide access to training courses, but don't actively look to grow their people personally and professionally. Having the processes in place to grow people will build teams of high performers. As people grow, so does the business as teams have focused goals and are rewarded for increases in productivity, innovation and CX.

- **Keep** great people. When they are being intentional about their workplace culture and have the processes in place to find and grow great people, SME owners reap the benefits of longer tenure. They have great people who are motivated, engaged and productive, and so over-deliver. This means the business owner can

INTRODUCTION

unstick themselves from the day to day and spend time focusing on growing their business.

The great part about putting in the HR frameworks for your workplace culture now is that they are scalable with your business. What works for a fifteen-employee business will work for 100 or 200 employees. You may have more resources available as you get larger, but the HR structure will grow with you. This means that as you scale up, you are not constantly chasing your tail to get great people performing and staying with you. Instead, you have a clear path for engaging and motivating your teams as they join your growth journey.

I'm excited to be sharing this methodology with you as you start your journey to create a great place to work. Are you ready?

PART ONE
DECIDING TO CREATE A GREAT PLACE TO WORK

There aren't many people in the world who wake up determined to have a bad day at work, annoy their co-workers and generally do a terrible job. Likewise, there aren't many business owners who hope to develop a workplace that employees dread coming to every day, but we know that these things do happen.

Deciding to create a great place to work needs more than intention. First, you need to understand what external and internal factors are impacting your business now or will impact it in the near future. This will help foster the motivation to be intentional about your workplace and create a great place to work.

1
External Drivers

You may have previously completed an analysis of your market and industry to understand your clients and competitors, but let's zoom up 10,000 km to look at external drivers. These are the pressures facing businesses across the world when it comes to survival and relevance.

It is important to reflect on how much the workplace has changed in the last few decades to understand the magnitude and pace of change to come. The words 'disruption', 'agile', 'pivot' which are now so commonplace would have been hardly referenced in workplaces years ago.

Perhaps your business hasn't felt 'big enough' to focus on HR, so you and maybe one or two other managers have been responsible for leading people and creating a great culture. The focus has been more on marketing, sales and finance, but if you think about it, for most businesses today, people are the competitive difference. The longer you wait to invest in HR, the larger risk you take that your employees will not be as productive, focused, loyal and motivated as they could be. This hampers your business in the best of times, but can be disastrous when major change hits.

The future of work

What was the workplace like when you first left high school or university? When I think back to my first job, I remember lining up outside the pay office every Thursday to be paid in cash. We didn't have personal computers, just a computer terminal with a black and green screen on which we could enter data, and then we'd print it off from a dot-matrix printer. All of our correspondence was done by fax and internal mail.

As employees, we had no access to management who seemed to lock themselves away in their offices. We had to clock in and out every day. Although smoking was illegal in the office by then, it was still socially acceptable and the senior managers had offices with ashtrays. They would happily smoke in their office after 5pm.

EXTERNAL DRIVERS

At the time of writing, this was not quite thirty years ago. Although this is a relatively short amount of time, we would not consider running a business like that today.

Management as a discipline dates back to the Industrial Revolution. There were terrible working conditions and an imbalance of power between workers and owners which gave rise to the trade union movement. Management practices created in the 1920s are still used today, but these methods are all about measuring everything employees do. In the last century, there was little trust or autonomy; micromanagement, bureaucracy and rules were the accepted tools to organise workers.

Here's a simplified way to look at the changes over a few generations.

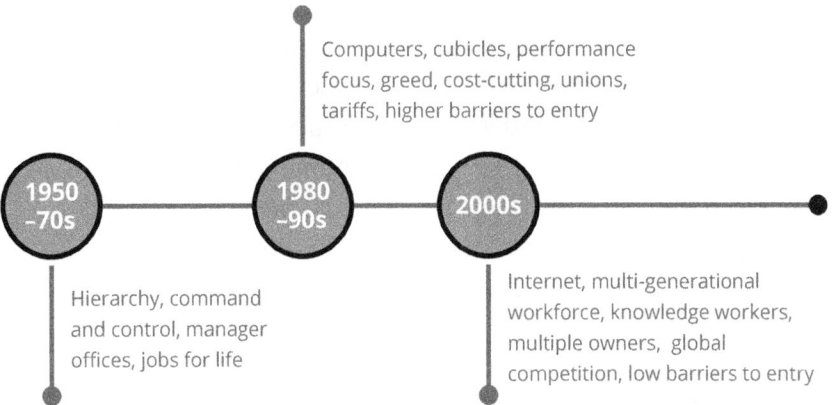

Industrialisation began over 100 years ago, but it has been since the 1980s that we have seen faster, larger and deeper change than ever before. We are currently in the fourth Industrial Revolution,[3] which is categorised by ongoing automation, particularly with the use of smart technologies. The 2020 World Economic Forum Future of Jobs report gives us a glimpse into the potential for the near future.[4] Automation of the workforce is happening faster than expected and the report predicts that by 2025, employers will divide work between humans and machines roughly equally.

The COVID pandemic accelerated changes to the workforce in 2020, forcing businesses around the world to close their offices and allow their employees to work from home. For years, office-based workers had been asking to have more flexibility, including working from home. Entire companies and divisions of consulting companies were created to teach other organisations how to manage a remote workforce, and conferences, books and presentations preached the benefits to leaders and HR practitioners, yet outside of start-ups and tech companies, prior to 2020, remote working seemed a difficult concept for organisation leaders to embrace. With technological leaps forward coinciding with change forced upon them by the pandemic, these leaders had to consider whether working from home or an office or a combination of the two would be the most productive option for their business.

EXTERNAL DRIVERS

In addition, it has become more difficult for businesses to succeed and remain relevant. An often-cited Boston Consulting Group study of 35,000 listed US companies in 2015 reported the average company lifespan has 'significantly decreased' from just over fifty-five years to fewer than thirty-five years.[5] The study found that almost one-tenth of listed US companies fail each year.

In Australia, the survival rate of businesses after four years is 64.5%. This may sound OK, but if I gave you 100 jellybeans and said that thirty-five of them could kill you, would you eat any of them? An interesting part of the Australian statistic is that the more employees the business has, the higher the survival rate, increasing to 78% with 5–19 employees and 82% with 20–199 employees.[6]

Another significant change to our workforce is the demographics. For the first time, we have five generations in the workforce at the same time. This brings challenges to the workplace as each generation can have a different approach to work, including what motivates them, how they communicate and what they are looking for from an employer. This will, of course, continue to change.

All these factors create significant challenges for today's business owners, but the good news is that great workplaces lead to high performance and growth, and long-lasting businesses. According to the

2020 Best Workplaces Australia study,[7] the businesses with fewer than 100 employees averaged over 70% revenue growth and have remained in business for over twenty years.

Today, there is a focus on employee engagement to get more productivity rather than productivity itself. Employee engagement means that employees bring their 'full selves' to work – they are enthusiastic, committed, care about the future of the company and are willing to invest energy into its success.[8] Focused and attentive to their work, they believe in the organisation's purpose. They don't just 'get things done'; they go above and beyond to achieve goals and are willing to put forward ideas and collaborate. They take less time off and attract and retain customers, thus increasing business profits.

Unfortunately, at the time of writing, engagement across organisations hasn't really changed over the last twenty years. According to Gallup, just 14% of workers in Australia and New Zealand are engaged – showing up every day with enthusiasm and the motivation to be highly productive.[9] Another 15% of employees are actively disengaged – not only unhappy at work but determined to undermine their colleagues' positive efforts. The remaining 71% of employees fall into the 'not engaged' category: they show up each day, but only do what is absolutely necessary to get through the day and no more.

This gives you a huge opportunity as a business owner. If you can create a great place to work with highly engaged employees, you're likely to gain a competitive advantage. You will be able to attract and retain great employees who deliver high customer satisfaction, productivity and profitability, all of which enable your businesses to thrive.

Disruption and transformation

There aren't many business owners I speak to who don't have digital transformation on the agenda. Some are even in the middle of a change program to digitise their processes.

For some business owners, this change has been forced upon them by an immediate need. For example, perhaps the technology they use won't be supported by the provider anymore. For others, it is an acknowledgement that without change, they will stop being relevant in the marketplace. The often-used examples of organisations whose leaders did not understand the future of their market and technological change are Nokia, Kodak and Blockbuster Video. No doubt there are thousands of SME owners who made similar decisions – or indecisions – which cost them market share or resulted in the closure of their business.

CASE STUDY: STAGEKINGS' STORY

Sometimes disruption isn't technological at all. I heard the word 'pivot' many times across 2020 and 2021 as businesses in industries decimated by the impacts of the COVID pandemic were forced to change or close their doors.

I particularly remember reading about Stagekings,[10] which was a live events company forced to stand down all its staff overnight when Australia went into lockdown in early 2020. Within just a few weeks, the leaders of Stagekings turned the company from one that decorated stages for large outdoor events (eg the Commonwealth Games opening ceremony, Formula One, Ninja Warrior) to one that created desks for people working from home.

I reached out to the founder and CEO, Jeremy Fleming, to ask him about his story because I couldn't help but wonder how an organisation would be able to pivot so completely if it didn't have people engaged and on board with the change. Jeremy told me about the organisation's devastating week in March 2020.

'There was a ban on all public gatherings from Friday 13 March which affected everything that we did and essentially cancelled all of our upcoming work immediately. We lost millions of dollars' worth of income the following week and we had to work out what we needed to do to stay alive. Part of that was realising we couldn't afford to keep any staff and we had to lay everyone off as there was no more work.'

Amazingly, the idea of creating desks for people working from home was born from this adversity.

EXTERNAL DRIVERS

Jeremy and his leadership team built an e-commerce site, and within three days, they had enough orders to reach out to some of the laid-off employees and ask them to come back to help cut and wrap the desks and deliver them all over Sydney. Before long, demand was so strong that not only did they bring their dozen staff back into the business, they hired an additional seventy.

The nature of the events industry dictates that employment is largely freelance and short-term contracting. This meant that during the lockdown, many people were out of work, but ineligible for government support. Jeremy and the team decided to support the industry by letting people know they had work available while donating over $100,000 in the first year to Support Act (an organisation that offers COVID-19 crisis relief grants to live performing-arts workers).[11] Stagekings didn't make huge profits during this time; it was simply focused on surviving, keeping everyone it could employed and supporting the industry.

Stagekings has always focused on employing people who fit within its culture, are engaged with the industry and want a workplace where they can have fun and variety while doing things differently. Imagine for a moment if Stagekings had employees who were managed as cogs in a wheel rather than valued as people. Would the staff have been open to completely changing the nature of their work? The company going in a new direction? I can imagine staff treated like that responding with, 'That isn't in my job description,' and at best begrudgingly returning to work. This is far from what Jeremy described:

'It was a really exciting place to be. It was quite a buzz for everyone to be in together and helping out.'

CASE STUDY: STREET SCIENCE'S STORY

Steve Liddell is the founder of Street Science, an Australian business which was developed with the vision to visit primary schools and get kids truly engaged in learning through student-centred hands-on experiments. Steve and his team of scientists and teachers would travel between schools in Southeast Queensland, and to science festivals both Australia-wide and throughout the world.

By the start of 2020, Street Science was in high growth mode – around 25% year on year. It was looking to expand when the pandemic hit and schools were closed. Although the full lockdown in Queensland only lasted around six weeks, external visitors, including Street Science, were locked out of schools for more like six months.

Street Science had a business model reliant on being in schools providing face-to-face programs for kids. Facing a complete shutdown of the business for an unknown period of time, Steve sought advice and learned that his best option was to make most of his team redundant, keeping just four staff – down from fourteen – to get through the period.

Steve told me, 'I said no, I'm going to keep every one of my staff. I decided I'd do whatever it took to keep my team and maintain the culture we'd built over the past five years. I'd been saying to staff that if they came to join us, they'd get work-life balance and stability in their job and, of course, they'd work and play hard. If I'd followed this advice, I would have been going against what I'd been trying hard to build and promising my staff.'

Steve and the leadership team had to create a plan because they had zero income for the foreseeable future, but they did have staff, leases and bills to pay. They decided that the business had a good presence in the community as before lockdown, it had been working with over 100,000 kids each year. As a team, they believe in education – wanting kids to love science – and supporting their staff. This combined to fuel the idea of creating a makeshift studio in their lab on day two of lockdown, purchasing some streaming software and producing live videos.

Steve said, 'We simply put it out there to the community and told people, "We're going to support you. We're going to take the kids off your hands for an hour every morning at 10am. They'll be engaged and learning, and with a bit of luck, this will give you a chance to have a cup of tea and get some work done without the kids running around under your feet."

'We taught science like we always do, with big fireballs and liquid nitrogen, but we also taught science that the kids could do at home.'

Although throughout this period, the business was not creating revenue, the pivot enabled Street Science to deliver on its core purpose of engaging kids in science. It also gave the team a feeling of job security and provided them with meaningful work.

Over time, the Street Science leaders created an online product called the Learning Lab, which is a paid subscription service. This required the team to change their core delivery model from classroom teaching to presenting in front of a camera. At first, many team members found it awkward and outside of their comfort zone, but they persevered because they were invested in the business.

In Steve's words, 'My team and I genuinely care about our staff. We want them to achieve their goals at work and grow as humans as well as grow within the business. They understand that as we've been able to communicate it.

'When it came to change like this, they could probably have pulled out a position description from two years earlier and said, "I don't do digital delivery, Steve", but I think they felt they owed it to the business because they're engaged members of a team, and we do a lot of stuff for them. Saying no wasn't really an option, and that's not because I said they had to. I truly believe that the culture we've created provides the environment where staff want to make stuff work because they care – and they do genuinely care.'

During 2021, I was discussing pivoting with other business owners and friends, and I found that there are completely opposite stories to those of Stagekings and Street Science. Some organisation leaders wanted to bring their employees back into the workplace, but the employees refused as they preferred to be stood down and receive the government support payments (which for some were more than their usual pay). I heard stories of employees complaining about having to do a different kind of work – or any kind of work at all – when the company wanted to pivot. This had short-term consequences as these companies were unable to adapt. In the long term, the consequences have become more serious as those businesses that could make changes now have a competitive advantage.

The experience of Stagekings and Street Science tells me that when employees believe in an organisation and its purpose, feel engaged and passionate, trust the owner and leadership team, and are rewarded and recognised for their work, the business as a whole finds it much easier to pivot, survive and thrive through disruption successfully.

Summary

A combination of leaps forward in technology, employee expectations, generational differences and unforeseen disruption means that the workplace is continually changing. These external drivers face all businesses, so to survive, founders and owners must consider them and how their business can continually adapt.

Focus and invest in your people and your workplace culture. This will enable your teams to come together through difficult times and your business to embrace changes and ultimately thrive.

2
Internal Drivers

Even if you aren't noticing any external drivers, chances are you have some internal drivers that are frustrating or concerning you right now. You may be feeling stuck in the day to day and too operationally focused. This is a common feeling for founders as the business grows, but much of the day-to-day work and decision making is still led from the top.

Perhaps key people are leaving your business and you are noticing a cycle of hiring and onboarding which is sucking resources and energy. There could also be a small voice in the back of your mind wondering if your compliance to employment legislation is where it should be.

It may even be a combination of these. All are important signals that it is time to focus on the HR frameworks and processes that will help your business to scale and grow.

Stuck in the day-to-day

I have worked with leaders who are frustrated as they can't get unstuck from the day to day. They are too operationally focused and attending too many meetings and too many 'HR issues'. This usually escalates when the business has around ten to fifteen employees and I have found two reasons for this.

The leaders started the business

Generally when a business begins, there is one founder, maybe two, with a business plan, a phone and a computer. The business may grow organically or receive funding, and then it's time to hire employees: usually some administrative support, then salespeople, then people to deliver the product or service, and so on.

What can be difficult in this process is that the owner/founder has generally been doing *everything* and it becomes hard to let go. They feel a connection to their customers and, particularly in service-based businesses, an obligation to be doing the client relationship management.

The leaders don't have the right team

Sometimes, the leader wants to remove themselves from the day to day and be strategically focused, but they can't get traction with the right team members to delegate to. Perhaps they have hired a general manager, but they haven't built the trust in them to delegate, or worse, they don't hire a second in command (2IC) at all and the team members are still reporting to the leader, which makes it impossible for them to focus away from operational matters.

The reason this is exacerbated at the ten- to fifteen-employee level – and it only gets worse as the business grows – is because this is the size where the span of control becomes too large for one leader. Ideally, each leader has seven direct reports, which can be increased to fifteen if all of those team members are doing the same job, but in a small organisation, it is more likely everyone will be in unique positions.

The shift from being stuck to being future focused is twofold. Firstly, the leader needs a mindset shift to accept that they can't do everything and if they try to, their business will eventually choke and fail. Secondly, the right structure and HR practices will enable the team members to be skilled, motivated and rewarded, which provides the leader with the trust to delegate to them.

I have worked with businesses where there is consistent feedback that the leader is a micro-manager. This creates a vicious cycle where great people leave because they don't have autonomy in their role, and the people who stay become disillusioned and continually gossip and complain. Unfortunately, this makes the micromanagement worse because the leader realises they can't keep the great people and the ones they have don't work as well as they should.

This creates risks to the business. It may receive a bullying complaint or workers' compensation claim, which in worst cases become prolonged legal battles. It is difficult for a small business to survive in these circumstances.

If you are feeling stuck in the day to day, this is the time to reflect on what is contributing to that. This book will give you the roadmap to implement great HR practices which will help, but you also need to shift your mindset and be ready to let go. It is not feasible for you as the owner or leader of a business to do everything, and if you try, you may experience not just burnout, but the loss of great people who don't feel like they have the ownership and autonomy to do great things.

Employee turnover

What is your employee turnover for the last year as a percentage? If you don't know the answer, that is not

INTERNAL DRIVERS

unusual, but I would encourage you to find out as it is a key metric for your business.

Employee turnover is costly. Depending on which article you read or person you ask, it can be anywhere from 30% to 200% of the person's salary, the wide range being reflective of the differences in costs associated with different types of roles. For example, the cost of losing a long-term employee with high levels of skills and knowledge is likely to be closer to 200%.

The direct and indirect costs of employee turnover include:

- **Hiring:** job ads, recruitment agency fees, psychometric tests, hiring manager time
- **Productivity loss** during the time of the vacancy and the time it takes for the new employee to get up to speed
- **Training** the new employee into their role
- **Morale:** employee turnover can have an impact on other team members, including reducing their productivity or encouraging them to look for a new job too

If I told you my employee turnover for the last year was 27%, would you think that is low, average or high?

Years ago, I worked with an organisation that had just received the results of its staff engagement survey. One of the results the senior management team was most surprised by was that almost 50% of employees had responded that they didn't think they would be working there in two years' time. From the managers' perspective, this was strange because the tenure in the organisation was good.

When I reviewed the employee turnover numbers, I saw the organisation had a history of over 25% for the last three years. Although the senior management may not have realised it, their employees were feeling the impact of one in four people leaving every year.

A simple way to calculate employee turnover is to take the number of employees who left in the last year (A), the number of employees at the start of that period (B) and the number of employees at the end of the year (C), then use this formula:

$$\frac{A}{(B+C)/2} \times 100$$

For example, if I had 8 employees leave the business this year (A), 27 employees at the start of the year (B) and 32 employees at the end of the year (C), my turnover would be calculated as:

$$8/((27+32)/2) \times 100 = 27\%$$

INTERNAL DRIVERS

To quantify this example, the average full-time adult ordinary-time earnings in Australia is $90,329 per annum.[12] Taking a conservative approach of the cost of turnover being 50%, that could mean that each person who left cost the business $45,164 of a potential total of $361,316.

Some business owners will take calculating employee turnover a step further and identify the percentage of resignations versus employer-initiated departures. That can be helpful if the business is slightly larger than the average SME, or if there was a redundancy program during the year which makes the turnover figures higher than usual.

Average turnover is reported every four years by the Australian Human Resources Institute. The 2018 report indicated businesses with 1–99 employees had the highest average turnover at 22%, and across all business sizes it was an average of 18%.[13] Most respondents considered the 'ideal' amount of turnover would be 1–10%. Personally, I have found organisations with less than 10% turnover can have their own challenges as there isn't enough movement to enable staff development and career paths. They also lose the opportunity to onboard new people to bring an injection of ideas and a fresh set of eyes to help prevent group think. From my perspective, 10–20% turnover is a better goal, but what is ideal for your business may be different.

When you have high turnover, it is difficult to gain traction on projects, which can damage your reputation with your clients, cause disruption and distractions to remaining staff, and impact the overall performance of the business. This is why employee turnover is considered to be so costly. If you are able to create a workplace that encourages great people to grow and stay with you, thereby reducing your employee turnover, that will make a huge impact to your bottom line.

Compliance

Most business owners want to do the right thing when it comes to compliance. Unfortunately, many of them bring experiences from the past which may not have been right to begin with, or the legislation has since changed.

CASE STUDY: WHEN GOOD INTENTIONS GO BAD

A business owner called me one day. He had a young apprentice who was having ongoing money trouble and the owner wanted to start a separate bank account for the apprentice in his own name, putting part of the apprentice's wages into that second account as forced savings. This had happened to the owner when he was an apprentice twenty years ago and he thought it was a great idea.

I explained to the owner that although he had good intentions, if he was to take part of his apprentice's wages and arbitrarily put it into a separate bank account

INTERNAL DRIVERS

that the employee couldn't access, that would be unlikely to be viewed as lawful. He could actually be seen as partaking in 'wage theft'.

Compliance is so important; you need to check any assumptions. Without the right foundations in place in terms of compliance with employment legislation, you're not going to be able to build a great culture. It is hard to sell your business as a great place to work if your employees aren't convinced their terms and conditions are right.

Lack of compliance often happens in SMEs because of a shortage of resources, but it can also impact large organisations. Uber discovered this when an employee, Susan Fowler, made a public post about sexual harassment and discrimination she experienced, which opened the doors to many other complaints revealing a toxic culture of bullying.[14] Co-founder Travis Kalanick resigned and his replacement, Dara Khosrowshahi, spoke at the end of 2018 about having spent his *entire first year* as CEO trying to rebuild the company's external image and internal culture, and settling lawsuits.

Woolworths is one of many large employers in Australia to be accused of wage theft.[15] This all came back to a hole in the company's processes which meant it wasn't properly checking that salaried staff were earning more than the modern award that covered them. Most businesses in Australia are covered by the Fair Work Act,[16] which provides the minimum terms and conditions of employment for employees, including the National Employment Standards and 122 modern awards ('awards'). These awards cover most occupations and industries, but this is the area I find most owners do not understand or apply correctly in their businesses.

Awards aren't just about pay rates; they also provide the minimum terms and conditions that apply to employees. What determines award coverage is your industry and the type of role someone does. Even if you are paying someone above the minimum rates, the rest of the terms of the award may apply, such as if it is allowable for an employee to cash out annual leave, the amount of notice to be given if your business is having an annual shut down and if annual leave loading is payable. The most common awards I find in service-based businesses are the Clerks Private Sector Award, which covers most administrative roles, and the Professional Employees Award, which covers many IT roles.

Here is a checklist that you can use as a starting point to make you aware of the base-level requirements for your business. What I am providing is general information that is not tailored to your circumstances, so please do not rely on it or use it as an alternative to legal advice. It is to encourage you to receive specific advice if you are unsure about the compliance status of your business.

Compliance checklist

- Which Modern Awards apply to your employees? How do you know? When did you last do a review?
- If you're paying salaries, how are you checking the employees are earning more than the award rate? How often are you reviewing this?
- Do all managers in your business understand the application of the awards (eg consultation, shutdowns, excess leave)?
- Do all employees have a written contract of employment?
- Do you have these policies in place? Have they been reviewed within the last two years?
    - Workplace behaviour (bullying, harassment, discrimination) including a complaints procedure
    - Code of conduct
    - Performance management
    - Leave
    - Working from home
    - Return to work program (workers' compensation)
    - Work health and safety (WHS) general policy

- Do you provide the Fair Work Information Statement and, for casual employees, the Casual Employment Statement to all new employees?

- Are you aware of the requirements to offer casual conversion to casual employees? Do you have a process that meets these requirements?

If you don't know the answer to any of these questions or the answer is no, these are the priorities for your business. These compliance areas can be reviewed and improved at the same time as you are embarking on a program to create a great place to work, as long as they are prioritised. If you don't fill the gaps, not only is it potentially a large risk for the business, it's also a major barrier to creating a great workplace culture.

Employment policies

Sometimes, I will hear business owners say, 'We don't want policies in our business, we don't want things to be that complex' or 'We don't want to be hierarchical and have red tape'. Those are valid concerns, but there are certain circumstances where a simple policy reduces the complexity for your business and gives everybody clear guidelines on how things are done in your workplace. On a day-to-day basis, policies help employees know how processes work and what the business expectations are, and give them a sense that everyone is treated equally.

INTERNAL DRIVERS

For example, a lot of businesses have moved to remote or hybrid working. As an employee, if I decide to move to Melbourne and you require me to come to Sydney every month for a team meeting, who pays for the travel? If you don't have some form of policy, you may get situations where some people are receiving different benefits to others, which causes feelings of inequity and unfairness across the business and reduces employee engagement.

If you are ever in the position where there is a claim against you as an employer, your policies will be reviewed by your lawyers and potentially the Fair Work Commission. If you don't have policies or they aren't clear, this can put your business in a difficult position.

There are certain policies I recommend for every business, no matter the size. One covers workplace behaviour such as bullying, discrimination, harassment and equal opportunity, along with the process for making a complaint.

If you don't have this policy in place and an employee discloses to you they felt uncomfortable in a certain situation, would you know what to do? In worst-case scenarios, they may make a complaint to an external body, and without a policy, you won't have clear steps on what to do next. Having a policy and following it enables everyone to be clear on the expectations in the workplace and what to do if those standards aren't being met.

You may think that this policy is common sense. Surely people know they can't bully, discriminate against or harass others, but we all continue to see examples in the media where people in organisations are engaging in this behaviour. It does still exist in the workplace, so it is better to be on the front foot than try to manage a major claim later.

A code of conduct is related to a policy, but expands further on what the expectations are in the workplace. For example, what happens if an employee starts a business directly in competition with yours or comes to work intoxicated or receives a significant gift from a client? This doesn't need to be a large and complicated document, but it is important to set the framework and expectations in place for everyone.

The remaining policies you need relate to WHS, working from home, leave and performance management. There are certain WHS policies that are required by all businesses and WHS obligations around employees working from home, so these documents and processes will keep you compliant. A leave policy is helpful as it touches every employee and sets out how and when they can apply for leave.

I recommend a performance-management policy because at some point, you're likely to have an employee who's not performing the way that you want them to. This policy enables managers in your business to know exactly what the steps are to manage performance (without which they may do nothing). It's also important for employees so they understand the process, which can reduce perceptions and accusations of bullying.

There may be other policies that are necessary for your business, such as travel, social media or remuneration. In most cases, around a dozen policies will cover most of your requirements. You can put these into one document, called an employee handbook, which provides a great basis for new employees to understand how your processes work. It can also be referred to as needed by current employees.

Summary

Are you feeling:

- Stuck in the day-to-day?
- The pain of great people leaving?
- Unsure about how well you comply with employment legislation?

These are key signals that you need to be more intentional about your HR practices and workplace culture.

Reflect on your willingness to let go, calculate your employee turnover rate and check your key compliance activities. Then you will be ready to build a great place to work.

PART TWO
BUILDING A GREAT PLACE TO WORK

Now you understand the external and internal drivers motivating you to be intentional with your workplace culture, it is time to build a great place to work.

You may feel concerned about stating this as your goal because you don't have the same resources as the big companies that shout to the world what a great workplace they have. Perhaps you are tempted to keep this goal to yourself and build some HR programs in the background rather than share it with the team.

Resist the temptation. This is an exciting time that is likely to make your team energised, motivated and ready to be a part of the journey. Sharing this vision with them is, of course, the first step to holding yourself accountable and believing you can create a great place to work.

Before you read on, take the quiz at www.findgrowkeep.com.au. The questions are designed to score you on the core areas described in this book and will provide you with a customised report based on your answers. It can help to have a starting point to reflect on around the areas your business has as strengths and where you may need to focus your attention.

3
Find

There is no faster or more impactful way to change culture than recruitment. A hire can quickly foster or infect a team, depending on whether you've made a great or bad choice, with long-lasting consequences. This is why it is essential to understand the type of culture and the structure your business is aiming for before you consider any changes to your recruitment practices.

Once you are clear on these pieces, then you can review recruitment with a marketing lens and actively and effectively sell your business as an employer to attract great people and ensure you are onboarding for success. Once you have the Find framework in place, recruitment stops being such a lottery and you can confidently bring great people into your business who not only fit your culture but thrive in it.

Your goal culture

When people think of workplace culture, many assume that high performance is the goal, but there are different types of culture. Although you want your people to be high performing, that may not actually be your goal culture.

I've identified four overriding workplace cultures: purpose, performance, innovation and customer. Once you know your goal culture, you can build the HR frameworks to support it, so let's have a look at each one in a little more detail.

Purpose culture

Although every business needs a clear 'why' or purpose, when I talk about a purpose culture, I mean a business that exists for a greater good. In other words, the purpose takes precedence over profit. Usually, these businesses have stable products or services, and innovation is driven by the need to stay relevant to the community that they serve. Often, I see a purpose culture with community-based, not-for-profit or charitable organisations and those in sectors like care for the aged and education.

Performance culture

This is all around having easily determined, set and managed metrics. Innovation is driven by competitiveness and wanting to be the best. There's a large focus on productivity and employees are rewarded for their achievement of clear performance measures. Usually, the business operates in a highly competitive market or industry, such as professional services.

Innovation culture

This culture focuses on idea generation, development and innovation. It's usually characterised by flat matrix-style structures where employees are encouraged to take risks and rewarded for innovation. These types of businesses compete in markets that undergo rapid change, such as the technology and pharmaceutical industries.

Customer culture

These businesses have frequent touchpoints with customers who are usually also the consumers of the product or service, so there's a philosophy of the customer's always right. Customers often give public feedback, so innovation is driven by better products and services. Businesses with a customer culture are often, but not always, business to customer (B2C) such as hospitality and retail.

As you read through the four goal cultures, you may have decided your business fits more than one. Perhaps it even fits all four. This is not unusual, but although you may want components of the others, it is important to decide on the *overriding* goal culture you want to achieve.

For example, Amazon workers are held to really high standards; the company even boasts that those standards are unreasonably high. Amazon uses data that allows individual performance to be measured continuously and an expectation that once employees 'hit the wall', they 'have to climb over it'.[17] There's no doubt Amazon has a strong focus on innovation and its customers, but the overriding idea of how it does things – its culture – seems to be performance.

This is important. Once you have determined your goal culture, then you can design all of your HR processes and practices around that culture. Along with your company values, you use the goal culture as a lens for important business decisions. You can also prioritise what will be important for your workplace culture, what may just be nice to have and what isn't important at all.

For example, innovative cultures encourage employees to research new product ideas, reward them for that research, send them to trend and future workshops, applaud risk taking and accept failure. They have systems for knowledge transfer and prioritise new methods and technologies for innovating.

A purpose culture accepts compassion as a valid reason to break a rule. Employees frequently share stories about the good that the business creates, while leaders encourage personal development in alignment with the company purpose and continually communicate to their customers and communities the value the business is providing to the greater good.

A customer culture encourages employees to give the right advice, even if that means referring a customer to a competitor. The leaders train their employees frequently in providing great service and products, and reward them for outstanding CXs.

A performance culture looks at the clear performance measures the business is using. Leveraging technology to manage or monitor that performance, it focuses on employee productivity and promoting people who demonstrate exceptional performance.

CASE STUDY: WE PLAY TOGETHER

Warren Carney is the owner of the brands Carney Sports Marketing, Classic Sportswear, Dina Uniforms and Primus Industries. The business collectively works under the slogan of 'We Play Together'.

I met with Warren and his senior leadership team and discussed the four cultures. Warren immediately said to me that his brands have a purpose culture, so I asked a lot of questions as I had expected it would be more of a customer or perhaps a performance culture. The answers Warren initially gave me were all related to the customer as his brands are more aligned with wanting to make their customers successful.

I then gave a hypothetical outline of what a purpose-based culture would look like. As a result, Warren told stories about how uniforms – sports or otherwise – can make everyone, no matter their background, feel good about their profession and ready to be successful. He explained that is what drives him and his business – the idea that anybody can feel good about being a sportsperson going out into the field of play or getting into a helicopter because they're a paramedic. It became clear as he was talking that purpose is the overriding goal culture, he is building a business with that culture in mind and it is driving the decisions that the business is making.

Just a few weeks later, when Warren's leadership team did a staff satisfaction engagement survey, in response to the statement, 'We are proud to work for this organisation', 100% of employees agreed or strongly agreed. When all your employees say they are proud to work for your organisation, that means you have a really strong purpose, you are communicating that to your staff, and they are on board with it.

Warren is a high-performing leader; he has a professional sports background and is always striving to be the best. He does that because his business's purpose culture and the passion that engenders drive him, and that has flowed through the organisation. This means he doesn't need to focus on a high-performance culture; it's considering how to continue to cultivate and embed the why of the organisation that inspires high performance in the team members.

Setting the structure

At inception, a business generally has one or two founders, and then as it grows, the founders add some administrative support, followed by employees to deliver the product or service. Over time, the structure gradually builds, but often not in any intentional way.

Often business owners I speak with have designed their structure around the employees' skills and desires. Perhaps at some point, they have picked up some tips on how to be more strategic and lift themselves out of the day to day from books like Gino Wickman's *Traction*.[18] These are completely valid things to do, but they are reactive.

Of course, you need to consider the reactive triggers for restructuring, such as:

- **Increase in sales.** Having a lot of work can be a great problem, but it means you may not have enough people to deliver your products or services. This is normally when a business owner decides to expand – you might hire a virtual assistant or other administrative support. In other words, when you can't actually deliver what you offer to your clients or customers, you bring on more staff, which effectively restructures your business.

- **Someone leaves.** Often you can't find a replacement in the market, which forces you to rethink the structure of your business and whether you need to change it. If an employee has gained skills, experience and knowledge during their time with you, it can be difficult to replace them, or the salary expectation of someone with the same skills might be much higher than you're willing or able to pay.
- **Employees complain.** You might restructure because a team member complains about having too much to do, so you hire someone else to help.

Taking a more proactive approach, let's look at five indicators which could prompt you to examine your structure.

1. Bottlenecks

These are a red flag that there's something going wrong in your structure. Bottlenecks come about when people feel:

- They aren't able to get on with their jobs
- They can't get things approved
- They don't get the information they need

For example, the sales team may be actively selling product A, but the marketing team is promoting product B. These situations can be really frustrating for the individuals in those teams as the salespeople feel unsupported by marketing and the marketing team members aren't seeing their efforts translate into sales. Bottlenecks result in the business not performing the way that it should be.

When this has happened with my clients, we've taken a look at the issue, asking the questions:

- Where are the bottlenecks?
- Why aren't the teams collaborating?

Often the knee-jerk response is, 'It's the fault of this person or that person'. A lot of the time, it's not actually one person but the structure that's at fault, so that's the best place to start.

Take a look at your team structure. Is there anything in it that is blocking collaboration or preventing a person from getting the information they need to do their job? It may not be that you need to hire a new person; the solution could be as easy as looking at the reporting lines. For example, someone may be reporting to the sales manager when they should be reporting to the marketing manager.

2. Lack of ideas and innovation

If you don't have ideas and innovation coming through to the senior management of the organisation, it may be another signal that you need to restructure. This usually happens for one of two reasons:

- **No time.** People are so busy, they don't have time to think about the future, better ways to do things, or better products or services to offer customers.

- **Communication.** People don't have the ability to get their ideas and innovations up to the right levels within the business.

A lack of ideas and innovation can stem from other things as well, such as poor leadership, no innovation opportunities such as brainstorming sessions, or ad-hoc reactive communication, but it's often an indicator of a need to restructure. To address this, put innovation on the agenda for your regular strategy meetings so your leadership team can discuss what ideas they have or are hearing from their teams.

3. Talent matrix

A talent matrix considers and categorises each employee according to their levels of performance and potential. Although this matrix comes into its own during succession planning and employee development, it is also helpful when you're considering the structure of the business.

The easiest way to do a talent matrix is to draw a square on a piece of paper. Then draw two vertical and two horizontal lines within it, so you end up with nine boxes. On one axis, write 'Potential', and on the other 'Performance'.

Place everyone on your team in the relevant box. When someone is high in potential and performance, they go in the top right box. When they're low in performance and potential, they go in the bottom left box.

			High potential and performance
Potential			
	Low potential and performance		
	Performance		

This gives you an organised way to review the people in your business and can prompt some close analysis:

- **High-potential and performance people.** Find ways to develop and retain them. For example, maybe they don't have any direct reports, so you may decide to make them a team lead to give them leadership experience. Alternatively, you may decide to give them exposure in another area that interests them, such as a temporary secondment, to keep them motivated.

- **Low-potential and performance people.** Where do they fit in your structure? Is there another role more suited to them or do you need to performance manage that person?

- **Everyone in between.** You could have people who are low in leadership potential, but medium or high in performance and are really good contributors. You may decide they're in the right spot in the structure or look at what could work better for them.

The talent matrix is a great process to do at least once a year and review quarterly, no matter the size of your business. It gives you a chance to pause and reflect on your team and identify where cross training and development opportunities may be (explained in more detail in Chapter 4).

4. Span of control

Keep an eye on how many people you're asking your team members to manage. In most cases, they should have no more than seven direct reports or, where there are multiple people in the same role, no more than fifteen. For example, a warehouse manager supervising fifteen store people who all do the same role is around the same level of complexity as an operations manager supervising seven people in completely different positions.

Once someone has more than seven (or fifteen) direct reports, this becomes really difficult for them to manage. As your business grows, it's easy to let this slide, particularly if you have a high-performing staff member managing the team. You may fall into the temptation of giving them everything – everyone is reporting through them and they're managing all the projects – but your star performer will then become overloaded. They'll start drowning, become disengaged and their high performance will evaporate because they have too much to do. When a manager's span of control gets to more than seven (or fifteen), it's time to look at your structure.

CASE STUDY: FREEING AN MD TO CONCENTRATE ON HIS JOB

I once worked with a client whose business had about a dozen employees. As managing director (MD), he found that he had no time for his 'day job' as most of his work was people management. Identifying this, he called in my business as HR support, but it became apparent that no matter how much support my team gave, the structure was inherently wrong.

The staff were mostly in the early stages of their career and needed high levels of managerial support. The MD's role was heavily focused around stakeholder management, which meant a significant amount of time out of the office and away from the team. He had one manager for part of the team so his span of control was on seven, but the nature of the business, his role and the team made this too large.

My team was able to amend the structure to include an operations manager to take on the people management and day-to-day tasks of the business. This enabled the business to run more effectively and the MD to keep the required external focus.

5. Strategic planning

You probably have a solid strategic plan in place that you revisit at least once a year, but do you consider your structure during this process? It's important to examine your organisation's triggers for taking on new staff and put this into your strategic plan.

For example, do you hire when you reach a certain:

- Percentage of revenue?
- Number of clients?
- Level of profit?
- Number of products that you're sending out the door?

Whatever it is, put the trigger in your strategic plan and use it proactively. For example, if you have one full-time employee (FTE) per $200,000 in revenue, when you reach $400,000, you'll need two FTEs, but you'll also need to plan ahead to staff up before you hit that $400,000. Your trigger point might actually be at $350,000 to give you time to get the employee in place.

The five indicators we've looked at in this section are about asking, 'How do I grow my business? What are the roles that I need? When do I need to review?' so you can be more proactive about your structure.

Recruiting great people

Most business owners I speak to give recruiting great people as their biggest challenge. There is no doubt that after years of low unemployment rates, skills shortages and the 'war for talent', it is not easy to attract great people.

Recruitment is the best opportunity we have to shape our business culture. A bad hire impacts on the whole culture, not just our reputation with potential and existing customers. The old saying 'hire slowly and fire quickly' is useful to reflect on. Often we are in a hurry to hire, so accept someone we aren't sure about, or we don't do our due diligence before offering them a role. That haste can really cost us.

Conversely, as soon as an employee shows signs that they are not a great fit, that is the time to decide to part company with them. Business owners often hesitate to act on problems with employees, though, because of the time and cost associated with recruitment, so someone who isn't performing or behaving in line with the culture stays much longer than they should, impacting on everyone around them.

Make learning how to recruit and onboard effectively your top priority so you can create and sustain a great place to work. This starts with understanding what you are offering the employment market.

Recruitment is much more of a marketing activity than an HR one. This may go against common opinion, so here's a simple explanation of how considering four basic stages of marketing can help you to attract great people.

1. **Creation of an offer.** Attracting candidates requires an offer that describes not only the job, but also your business as an employer.
2. **Research and testing.** If you are describing your business as having a 'great culture', how do you prove this? Conduct research with your current employees on what is great about working in your business and include this feedback in your advert. (More on this in Chapter 5.)
3. **Advertising.** Consider the ad copy and the best channels to use in advertising the vacant role.
4. **Selling.** Developing your employer brand and effectively selling your organisation and the role will be key to your recruiting success. Have you heard the saying 'You never get a second chance to make a first impression'? This applies to you as an employer as much as it does to the candidates you are interviewing and employees you are hiring. From your job ad through the recruitment

process to day one, that employee is sizing you up. Even if you don't make that all-important good impression, they may still take the job, but only until 'something better' comes along. This can lead to high turnover or employees going through the motions, but not being as engaged or productive as you had hoped.

Position description (creation of an offer/ research and testing)

Before you take any recruitment steps, it is important to be super clear on what the purpose of the role is. Creating or updating a position description before you go to market will enable you to get clarity before hiring. These documents are also extremely useful in helping the new employee to understand the expectations of their role, and to create goals and key performance indicators (KPIs).

There are four principles when it comes to position descriptions.

1. Clarity

A position description helps you and whoever is recruiting for the role to have clarity over the purpose of the position, and the skills, knowledge and experience that an ideal candidate would possess. It means that once an employee is hired, you have a common understanding of the expectations for them in the role.

Start with considering what the purpose is of this role. Stay away from motherhood statements, instead making this description as specific as possible. For example, for a sales manager position, if the purpose of the role is described as 'To create great experiences for our customers and showcase our products', that's too high level and doesn't get into the core of the job. Instead, if the ad describes the role as 'To create and implement the sales cycle for XYZ Company and achieve the yearly revenue targets', it will leave candidates in no doubt as to what they're applying for. Remove any jargon from the role description, and if you are using initials or acronyms, provide a definition.

A great way to test the position description is to give it to a friend or a family member and ask them if they understand what the position entails. If somebody outside of your business can read the document and be quite clear on the purpose of the role and why it exists, then you know that you have clarity.

2. Keep it simple

Too many times, I have seen position descriptions that are more like a long laundry list of tasks. Some employers believe that if they don't include a task in the position description, the successful candidate won't have to do it. Not only is that generally not true, but it's also old-school management.

You will have an overriding purpose for the role, so be clear on the key accountabilities, keeping these to between five and eight. A key accountability is something that will take up at least 10% of the successful candidate's time.

Let's use the sales manager as an example again. If they will talk once a month to the marketing manager and get some social media statistics, then that's not a key accountability. The key accountability may be that every month, they will generate reporting which includes those types of statistics.

Describe each key accountability in two to three sentences that start with an action word such as achieve, arrange, build, invent, launch, evaluate, guide, provide or recommend.

3. Review for bias

Bias is the sometimes unconscious tendency to treat people unfairly due to a deep-seated belief that certain traits make some people better than others. It is vitally important to write a position description for the role and not for the person, so remove any content that may be seen as bias towards particular groups.

This may seem obvious, but there are organisations that still use gendered position titles such as storeman. Perhaps a less obvious example is around age, which comes up when a position requests a certain number of years' experience. The problem with this is that it can unconsciously bias you regarding the type of person you're looking for in the job. It is better to be open-minded about the 'right' candidate as they can come from all manner of different experiences and skillsets.

CASE STUDY: WHAT'S REALLY IMPORTANT?

Recently, I had a discussion with a hiring manager. His position description said 'significant experience' in a particular area, but he wanted it to specify a number of years. I asked him to imagine he had two candidates: one had two years' experience in that area and all of the other requirements, the other had ten years' experience, but not all of the other requirements. Would the first candidate's lack of experience matter?

He thought about it and agreed that it wouldn't be a deciding factor. This enabled a great discussion around what the most important parts of the role were and how we could look for transferrable skills and experience in the hiring process.

---

4. Review process

There aren't many companies that are good at scheduling the reviewing of position descriptions to make sure they stay up to date. The easiest way to have a process for this is to review the position descriptions every time you advertise a job. Then at least once per year as part of the goal setting process, review them again. This will keep position descriptions as live documents that can help in situations that may need performance management.

Employer brand (research and testing/selling)

To attract the right candidates, consider your employer brand, which means looking at the target market for your job vacancy. If you have conducted an employee satisfaction and engagement survey, this can also provide excellent insights into how to market yourself as an employer.

Your goal culture is a good place to start when you're developing your employer brand. If the business has a performance-based culture, then you need to attract employees who are motivated by goals and achieving targets. If it's a purpose-based culture, then you are looking to attract like-minded people who share your purpose and want to serve your community.

CASE STUDY: WHY AN EMPLOYER BRAND IS IMPORTANT

My team and I worked with a training and development company whose leaders decided that it has a performance-based culture. When we did the staff survey, it became clear through the question responses and open comments that this is a fast-paced business where employees love to achieve, work hard and be creative, but they also care about each other and their customers.

This narrative enabled us to create an employer brand which the leadership team could use in job ads, interview questions and onboarding. Not only does it help the business to filter in the right kinds of candidates (and filter the wrong ones out), but it gives a realistic picture of the organisation and the culture to the candidates before day one.

Your target market in the context of potential employees has two attributes: it is a match for your goal culture in terms of motivations and values, and it is a skills match for the specific job you are hiring for. It is imperative to be clear on your target market before advertising, but be open-minded. Most business owners would love experienced staff, but if the role you need to fill doesn't require those qualifications, then broaden your scope.

For example, a retail business needs staff to work at modern award rates in a store. Training is minimal, perhaps taking four hours; what the employee really needs to be is friendly, approachable, trustworthy and reliable. In this situation, the business needs to advertise for and shortlist people with these qualities and values rather than experience.

Job ad (advertising)

Make sure your job ad reflects the personality of your business, which means considering your values and writing an ad that is aligned to those. This gives the job seeker a good idea of what you are looking for *and* what you reward.

For example, if your organisation is an entrepreneurial one that has an innovative goal culture, make the ad creative. Give candidates a puzzle to solve before they can send in an application or ask screening questions so candidates can show how they foster ideas and innovation.

Too often, I see a job ad which follows this formula:

- **Company name.** Perhaps a sentence or two about the organisation.
- **The role.** What the employer wants and what a candidate needs to bring to the table.
- **The role responsibilities.** A list of everything the employer will expect the candidate to be able to do in the role.
- **Skills and experience.** A list of what the candidate needs to possess for the employer to consider them for the role.

It then closes with:

- Previous applicants need not apply.
- Only shortlisted candidates will be contacted.

Have you noticed something about this formula? The ad is all about the employer and what they are looking for. Even worse, point one is often missing and the ad is listed on job boards as 'Private Advertiser', so the candidates have no idea who the employer is. Imagine trying to sell a product or service by using an ad that doesn't speak at all to your customers. There is a reason the business is readvertising.

Instead, consider the candidate as the customer and design a job ad that will attract, inform and filter in the right applicants. This advice will help:

- **Visual and informative.** Make the job ad visually attractive as well as informative. Colour and images really do catch the eye if the platform you are using enables them.
- **Contact person.** Always include a contact name, phone number and email address. Passive job seekers are unlikely to send their resume through to an anonymous job board form; they probably have questions they would like answered first.
- **Update LinkedIn.** Many potential candidates will 'stalk' the contact name on LinkedIn while deciding if they want to work for the company, so make sure your leadership team's LinkedIn

profiles are up to date and accurately reflect your business purpose and culture.

- **Candidates can also be potential customers.** Including sentences in your job ad like 'only shortlisted candidates will be contacted' is old-fashioned and kind of rude. There is no excuse for this in today's world; even if you use a template email, you can easily let someone know they have been unsuccessful. Remember, that job seeker could be a potential customer or a friend or relative of an existing employee. Make sure every interaction builds your company's brand in a positive way.

- **Use the right recruitment agency.** If you are using a recruitment agency, then use the right one for the job. You will spend a significant amount of money employing an agency expert, so find one who has experience in your industry and ask to see the ad copy before they post it so you can be sure you're happy with the content.

- **Make it easy to apply.** This is particularly important if you're hiring for a position which is difficult to fill in the marketplace. Requirements in the job ad such as 'Only applications with a cover letter will be considered' may prevent you from hearing from a great candidate who is busy, so decides to apply for other roles which just require the click of a button.

- **Less is more.** Keep your job ads clear and concise. Sell your company in the initial paragraph, provide brief information on the role, and then explain the type of candidate you are looking for and any qualifications they require.

It is important to consider if the role title you are using internally translates to the external market. Sometimes it is worth advertising the role with a title that is more generic so that you attract the right candidates and the ad will be picked up in job searches.

For example, what do these titles mean to you:

- Partnerships, culture and client manager?
- Licensing manager?
- Information technology services manager?
- Education coordinator?

How about:

- Practice manager?
- Stakeholder ad relationships manager?
- Technology projects manager?
- Events and partnerships coordinator?

These are all examples of where the original titles attracted candidates who did not match the role. On changing the role title for the ad to the equivalent in the second list, the employer was able to get applicants much more aligned to the position.

Let's have a look at an example of a job ad designed to attract great people.

JOB AD EXAMPLE: Marketing Assistant

About the team:

We run a consulting company that specialises in helping businesses of around 10–100 employees create great places to work so they can scale up and grow.

Since starting in 2016, we have developed our 'Find, Grow, Keep' methodology which enables businesses to create a workplace that attracts, grows and keeps high-performing and engaged teams. This forms our key service offering: a twelve-week HR program which builds culture, creates and aligns HR processes, rewards great performance and measures key areas consistently.

We are a small and committed team who believe in business for good and tie our everyday activities to charitable giving.

We value:

- **Being human.** We are all human. Compassion, gratitude, respect and fun are all welcome.
- **Continual learning.** We strive to grow personally and expand our expertise, which enables us to provide the best outcomes to our clients.

- **Trusted partnerships.** Trust is built in the small moments that we have with each other and our clients. Openness, collaboration, teamwork and coaching start here.
- **Get stuff done (GSD).** We are reliable, take initiative, work ethically and GSD.

About the role:

You will be working closely with the business owner, proactively and systematically completing administrative tasks that help the company achieve its marketing goals. You are not required to provide marketing strategy, copywriting or design, although your ideas are always welcome.

Task examples:

- Manage the marketing calendar and content production processes.
- Coordinate content creation and publication with copywriters and podcast guests.
- LinkedIn sales navigator – create lead lists and communications.
- Create, send and optimise email campaigns.
- Run ad campaigns on social media platforms.
- Social media scheduling and management.

This is a part-time role where you are free to set your own days and times of work, up to twenty-four hours per week. We will provide the technology required, but you will need a dedicated space to work from home.

About you:

- You've always been a 'doer' who likes to plan and GSD.
- You want to feel valued and respected, and work as part of a team.

- You're enthusiastic, love to support others and do great work.
- You enjoy technology and learning new platforms.
- If you don't know how to do something, you search out the answer and shout out if you can't find it.

Next steps:

If this sounds like you, apply now at careers@amplifyhr.com.au, or for more information, contact *name* at *phone*.

Interviewing process

A pre-interview telephone conversation is the best way to start this process, which means you and the candidate are both investing about fifteen minutes of your time. This gives both parties an opportunity to understand what the other is offering and if there is a potential match.

Use the telephone interview to ask why the candidate applied for the role, what they are looking for in their next position and where they are in their job search. Give them some basic information around the position, particularly the role's hours, days, location and any 'non-negotiables' (for example, working one Saturday per month). This enables both you and the candidate to work out if the job is a potential fit before moving to a formal interview where you explore their skills and experience more, and they learn more about you, the company and the role.

When you and the candidate are ready for the formal face-to-face or video interview, give thought to the type of questions you will be asking. Make most of your questions behaviour-based and align them to the purpose, vision and values of your organisation.

Behaviour-based questions are those which give candidates a specific example of a situation and ask about when they have encountered a similar situation. For example, 'Tell me about a time when things didn't go to plan. What happened?' Past behaviour is an indicator of how someone would perform in the future.

Let the candidate know you are looking for three components in their answers:

1. The *situation* or *task* leading to the candidate's actions
2. The specific *actions* they took or did not take
3. The *results* or *changes* caused by these actions

Candidates appreciate professional, structured interviews, so how you conduct this important step says a lot about your organisation. Design standard questions prior to interview. For the candidate, this helps them to feel that it is a fair interview and provides them with a positive experience. As the interviewer, you can stay focused and on track, so you can evaluate each candidate objectively, compare candidates and keep on time in interviews.

Examples of behaviour-based questions:

- Describe a specific time when you coached an employee. What was the impact?
- Would you provide an example of when you improved CX?
- What happened when you were faced with a situation that was extremely frustrating?
- Describe a time on any job that you've held in which you were faced with problems or stresses that tested your coping skills. What did you do?
- Give an example of a time in which you had to be relatively quick in coming to a decision.
- Tell me about a time in which you had to use your verbal communication skills to get a point across that was important to you.
- Give me an example of a time when you were able to build motivation in your team.
- Provide an example of a time when you had to go above and beyond the call of duty to get a job done.
- Describe a time when you felt it was necessary to modify or change your actions to respond to the needs of another person.
- What did you do in your last job to contribute to a positive team environment?

Pre-employment psychometric tests

Although structured behaviour-based interviews are important, they do have limitations. One is bias, which can come in many forms. Although we may consider gender, ethnicity and age, we often have other biases, including perceived beauty. One study found that 62% of managers will select an attractive applicant as their first choice.[19] A separate study found that a candidate having a scar or a stain on their face distracts the interviewer and leads to the candidate being rated lower than the others.[20]

Another limitation is impression management or 'faking'. Candidates want to make a good impression and will become highly skilled and practised in answering interview questions, which doesn't necessarily translate to job performance.

Because of these limitations, to get the best outcomes, use appropriate psychometric tests as part of the recruitment process. Analysis conducted by organisational psychologists looking at 100 years of research into recruitment has found that the best predictors of job performance are cognitive tests.[21] Including these with structured interviews is the way to select a candidate who can learn and get up to speed fast.

In addition to cognitive tests, if the role is a senior or leadership position, you may include other behaviour-based or emotional-intelligence tests. These, along with the interview, provide great insights and predictive information to consider to make the best choice of candidate.

Job offers

The marketing role doesn't end with a job offer. Now the candidate is a new employee, you need to make sure you do what you can to prevent 'buyer's remorse'. Make the job offer personal and give the successful candidate lots of praise and congratulations. Tell them how excited you are. In other words, make the offer process as positive as possible.

Whatever you can do to stay in touch with the new employee between the offer and the first day is a bonus. Are they in a leadership role? Send them a book on leadership that you use in the business or one that you like personally. Do you have a product-based business? Send them some free samples. This gets not only them excited, but also their friends and family, cementing their belief that they've made a great decision to join your business.

Onboarding for success

CASE STUDY: A TALE OF TWO ONBOARDINGS

All names and identifying features have been changed in this case study to protect anonymity.

A few years ago, my friend Fiona started a new job. Fiona arrived on-site at her workplace on her first day – it was a secure site so employees needed keys to gain access. Her new colleague Kim met her outside and took her into an office where Fiona left her handbag, including her mobile phone, before Kim took her for a tour around the site.

While they were outside, a car pulled up driven by another employee, Harry. Kim waved at Harry and they had a brief conversation while Fiona stood a few metres away and waited politely.

To Fiona's dismay, Kim hopped into Harry's car and yelled out, 'I won't be long, we just need to nip to Bunnings to get some supplies,' and then Harry drove off. Fiona was left outside, locked out of the building with no belongings. She didn't even know Kim's surname or where her office was (with her bag and phone inside), so felt that she couldn't go to the door and ask someone to let her in without seeming stupid. Instead, she decided she had no option but to find a place to sit and wait – for almost an hour – until Kim returned.

Imagine how you would feel being Fiona. Compare this to Ann starting a new office job.

On her first day, Ann's new team left a welcome card and small gift on her desk. Her computer was set up with the programs she needed and she was assigned a buddy to get her started with her day. Her new manager took her out for lunch, provided her with insights into the company's culture, including background on the leadership team, and answered all her questions.

Consider how Ann and Fiona each felt on their first day. The dismissive and thoughtless behaviour from

Kim continued, so you may not be surprised to learn that Fiona left the job within a year. In contrast, Ann felt welcome and an immediate sense of belonging and commitment to her new job.

When you find great people, it is your responsibility to make sure that they are welcomed and both their head and their heart are engaged. Simply showing someone their workspace and wishing them well is not going to give them a sense of belonging or a clear idea of what you expect from them.

What actions you take, or don't, in an employee's first few days and months will stay with them throughout their whole career with your company. Most people have no problems recalling their first day in a job, more so when it is a poor experience. These experiences become company lore and get brought out at focus groups and engagement surveys, even years later.

Onboarding reinforces the employee's decision to join and helps ensure they don't get feelings of 'buyer's remorse'. Consider some of the benefits of a structured onboarding program:

- 70% improvement in productivity[22]
- 54% higher employee engagement[23]
- 97% increase in productivity from employees assigned a 'buddy'[24]

Gallup reports that only 12% of employees strongly agree their organisation does a great job of onboarding.[25] Most programs are focused on process and paperwork rather than trust, communication and collaboration. This is why a structured onboarding process is critical to differentiate your business from other employers, and it doesn't need to be complicated.

Before day one

There may be weeks between when a new employee is interviewed and when they start with your business. During this time, the employee will probably be feeling excited, but also quite anxious. You want to do what you can to reduce buyer's remorse and keep them excited and eager to join.

Use this time to set the employee up with everything they will need, such as computer logins, office passes, computers, uniforms, etc, for their first day. Communicate to the broader business that a new starter will be coming on board, select a buddy for the new employee and schedule a time for them to meet on day one.

Send the employee a letter before their first day, welcoming them and congratulating them on their new role, and organise a new employee gift pack. This can be a mixture of company marketing/promo materials (to create a sense of belonging) and other treats (to create a sense of value).

If the employee is starting remotely, include the gift pack with the welcome letter. If they are coming into the office, make it available for them on their desk on the first day.

Ideas for the gift pack:

- Chocolates
- Notebook
- Complimentary welcome coffee at the local cafe
- Mints
- Promo goods (mug/mousepad/pens)
- Last employee newsletter and customer newsletter
- Book – for example, if there is a leadership book that is reflective of the culture you are striving to achieve, this is ideal for a new manager, or for a new team member, a book around customer success philosophies

Day one

The manager meets and greets the new employee and shows them around the office (if applicable), introducing them to their team and key contacts. The manager or buddy then completes an onboarding checklist, which includes WHS and other 'good-to-know' information, such as how to book the meeting room. If they'll be working remotely, the employee needs information around ergonomics, so their manager will discuss with them any issues they may have with their home workspace.

The role of buddy is designed to ease the new employee's transition into the organisation. The buddy is chosen by the manager, usually from the same team, to help new staff members make their way through their first few months with the organisation. Having a friend in the workplace is a key factor in employee engagement, so choosing the right buddy is important.

Buddies significantly impact a new employee's first impressions of the organisation. The buddy helps the new staff member understand how the organisation operates and the correct procedures and key processes to follow. They are an essential point of contact in the team for the new staff member.

The first few months

During the first month, the manager:

- Explains the company purpose and goals to the new employee
- Sets performance goals with the employee for their probation review
- Organises relevant networking/meet-and-greet appointments for the new employee

- Has regular check-ins with the new employee

The buddy:

- Notifies the manager of any induction issues or problems
- Completes the buddy checklist

At around month three, the new starter will complete the first-impressions survey (see Chapter 5). This is a good time for the founder or CEO to have coffee with the new employee if the business has fewer than around forty employees. Although the manager won't have check-ins with the new employee as frequently after month three, this is a good time to discuss how often to set up regular one-to-ones. At month five, the manager and employee complete the probation review process and set new goals/objectives for the coming year.

Structured onboarding leads to a productive employee with a long-lasting positive impression of the organisation. It is a great opportunity to demonstrate that you have considered the new employee as a person, not just a resource. New starters will share their initial employee experience with their family, friends, ex-colleagues or on socials, which – if the experience is positive – reinforces your great employer brand.

Summary

You've now been introduced to the first part of the Find, Grow, Keep methodology. You are aware of the goal culture you are looking to achieve, know how to review your structure proactively, and how to design recruitment and onboarding practices to attract great people who are motivated and excited to be a part of your team. Next, you need to build the HR practices and processes to grow your people so you can grow your business.

4
Grow

I have often heard people say, 'Employees don't leave their jobs, they leave their managers.' While this has a ring of truth, it isn't the only reason people leave businesses.

Expectations on leaders have changed dramatically over the last few decades and will continue to do so. This makes leadership development and the ability for leaders to be flexible in their thinking priorities in any business. Employees also need to feel they are growing in their roles, which means them having goals to achieve, being rewarded for performance and receiving structured development.

Business owners can often overlook the importance of internal communications, but having a structured plan in place will help to keep everyone informed, excited and motivated to achieve. With all these components in place, you can be intentional about growing your people to create a great place to work.

Growth and development

There's an uncredited quote that I have seen many times:

> 'The CFO asks the CEO, "What happens if we invest in developing people, and then they leave us?"
>
> 'The CEO responds, "What happens if we don't and they stay?"'

I love this quote. It reminds us all to consider the people who mentally checked out a long time ago, but still work in our businesses. Have you ever had an employee like that? The resulting effect is a productivity decline which can sometimes spread dysfunction across the whole team.

Many business owners and leaders I speak to aren't sure how to develop employees, especially when their business is small and still growing. It is important to remember that development is not just about the next job or career change; it's about keeping great people who are interested in continually learning in their current roles. Growth and development are key components of employee retention, so don't put them to the side because you think your business is too small or you just accept that new employees will leave every few years.

Consider the research that shows growth and development are top priorities when it comes to keeping great people:

- Hays found career progression and training opportunities, along with flexible work, are the top three benefits employees value.[26]
- According to LinkedIn, 94% of employees said that they would stay at a company longer if it invested in their career development.[27]
- Gallup found that 87% of millennials consider professional development or career growth important.[28]
- Another report by LinkedIn tells us that 76% of millennials believe learning is the key to a successful career.[29]

Even in small businesses, there are simple ways to encourage growth and development that don't mean employees need to attend expensive training every month. It's about identifying key areas that are important to the employee *and* help your business by broadening their mindset, industry contacts and knowledge.

I find the best ways to encourage growth and development in SMEs are:

- Structured development plans
- Guidance on simple development ideas
- Talent matrix process
- Program of workshops

Structured development plans

If you are having performance discussions with your employees quarterly, this is the perfect opportunity to incorporate simple development plans which are also reviewed quarterly. Part of this process is asking your employees what you can do to help them, how you can give them more meaningful work and what you can delegate to them.

As the employee develops, they will become more efficient, which frees up time for them to take on more duties that in turn continue to strengthen their skills and experience. This 'chain reaction' of progress organically feeds into your business having a highly productive team.

Each quarter, encourage your team members to select a development goal. Agreeing one goal per quarter not only helps them to grow, but cements development as a key part of your culture. The development goals could be as simple as:

- Identifying a mentor
- Listening to a TED talk every month
- Joining a networking group
- Shadowing other team members

Selecting one goal per quarter is achievable, and over time you can build upon this. For example, if an employee is reading a business book this quarter, then next quarter they could give an overview of that book to the whole team, including the key takeaways and ideas that you can implement within your team.

Guidance on simple development plans

I've come across employees who have no interest in creating a development plan and this can be difficult to manage. Often, I find it is because they don't understand that development doesn't necessarily mean a training course or changing careers. Examples of on-the-job development ideas in a document on a shared drive or in a nicely designed *My Career* booklet can help not only to show that growth and development are important, but to provide a platform for creating a development plan.

Some on-the-job development examples include:

- Volunteer to present a 'lunch 'n' learn' regarding a goal or objective you have achieved or something you have learned.
- Prepare a business case for expenditure, including how the team and organisation will benefit from it.
- Identify three major opportunities and three major risks for your area(s) of responsibility. Based on this, develop a plan to help ensure the opportunities are realised and the risks avoided. Present/discuss this plan with your manager.
- Develop and implement a questionnaire which would help you speak to an internal/external customer to find out their real needs.
- Contact at least a couple of the people on whom your role impacts and find out their perception of your role and how it can best serve them.
- If you are writing a report, consider how you would convey the same information as a presentation; if you are delivering a presentation, consider how it would look written as a report. This will increase your skill and flexibility.
- Write a newspaper headline for the report or presentation. This will help you to identify for the recipients what the single main message is.

- Draw up a flowchart of how your role impacts other areas, and vice-versa. Find out about any of the areas you don't already know about.
- List at least three people within and outside of your organisation whom you want to learn from. Beside each name, list the topic that you want to discuss, and then reach out to those people.
- Substitute for your manager in meetings or while they're on leave.

It is commonly held that 70% of development activities should be on the job, 20% through relationships with others (eg feedback, networking, coaching) and only 10% through structured courses. Defining this, along with examples of on-the-job development, helps you to set the scene of what development plans look like. Although each employee is ultimately responsible for their own development, your team members don't know what they don't know, so it is important for you as a leader to guide and help them with ideas.

Talent matrix process

I introduced the talent matrix in the 'Setting the structure' section of Chapter 3. Not only is it a great way to be proactive with your structure, it will also help you identify the employees who have the most potential to be invested in.

Potential		C – Needs development	B – Meets expectations	A – Exceeds expectations
1	High	• New in position or wrong fit for role?	• Individual development plan • Prioritise for training $ • Include in leadership workshops	• Individual development plan • Prioritise for training $ • Include in leadership workshops • Career conversations
2	Moderate	• Coaching • May lead to performance management	• Individual development plan • Include in leadership workshops	• Individual development plan • Prioritise for training $ • Include in leadership workshops
3	Low	• Performance management	• Continue to motivate, reward and recognise	• Continue to motivate, reward and recognise

Performance

Boxes A1, B1 and A2 contain those who are high in potential and meet/exceed performance expectations, or exceed performance and are moderate in potential. For these employees:

- Encourage individual development plans
- Prioritise budget for training courses
- Include in leadership workshops

You may also hold career conversations with these people, particularly those who are high in potential and exceeding performance expectations (A1). More information on this is available in the 'Career paths' section of Chapter 5.

You may not prioritise B2 – the employees who meet expectations and have moderate potential – for external training, but they need an individual development plan and to be included in leadership workshops. High-potential and low-performance people – box C1 – may be new into the role or the role may be the wrong fit. If they're new into the role, give them support, tools and development to succeed. If there is a fit issue, review the role and potentially redesign it or find a more suitable role for the employee.

Where an employee's potential is moderate and their performance needs development – box C2 – focus on uncovering the reasons for the performance gap. This requires coaching and asking open questions, but if there is no improvement, these employees may need performance management.

Employees with low potential who meet or exceed performance expectations – boxes A3 and B3 – are often the engine room of small businesses. They tend to love their job and not be interested in career development. It is vital to motivate, reward and recognise these employees, but continue to check that their circumstances haven't changed in regards to developing into a new role.

Employees with low potential and low performance – C3 – need performance management. The aim is to provide them with the support and development to improve, but if this improvement doesn't occur, consider disciplinary action. This may include termination of employment.

Conduct this exercise once per year and review it at least half-yearly. This will help you maintain the momentum of growth and development with your teams.

Program of workshops

You may have noticed on the talent matrix that four boxes state to include their people in leadership workshops. The first step is to confirm with the employee that they are interested in leadership development. If they are, rather than inviting them to find their own leadership training courses, speak to a facilitator or HR consultant about how to create a small program of workshops across the year. This program of workshops, which is named, enables excitement among your employees who acknowledge it as being of great benefit to them rather than a scatter-gun approach to individual training sessions. You can do this with as few as five employees.

CASE STUDY: IGNITE

My business had a client who identified six employees in the top right four boxes of their talent matrix. We decided that those employees, along with anyone who was currently a manager of people, would be invited to attend leadership workshops. Scheduling in one workshop for a half day each quarter, we named the program 'Ignite'.

We then had some special invitations made that told the employees they would be joining the company's leadership program that year. This gave them a sense of excitement while recognising their status as leaders in the organisation. Having everyone in one group had the additional benefit of increasing communication and collaboration, and the participants cited getting to know their colleagues as a key benefit of the program.

When you design a program this way, you can form accountability groups. These are groups of two to three participants who agree to meet in between each workshop and have specific homework to complete between the sessions. This helps not only embed the learning, but also build relationships cross functionally.

Leadership today

As we saw in Chapter 1, the workplace has changed significantly and continues to do so. What we possibly considered good leadership five or ten years ago may now fail to motivate our teams. I often hear that just being a manager isn't good enough; we all need to strive to be continually developing as leaders.

There is a difference between being a manager and a leader. Being a leader is not about your position in a hierarchy; it is about your behaviour and actions. Demonstrating leadership can mean helping teammates move through change positively, implementing new processes to improve your customer outcomes or providing considered ideas to impact the future of the organisation. Being a manager is hierarchical and related to the mechanics of managing people, for example organising work, approving leave, delegating, following processes and managing budgets.

Simon Sinek, a well-known global speaker and author, states on leadership:

> 'Others willingly follow you – not because they have to, not because they are paid to, but because they want to.'[30]

The definition and expectations of leadership are continually changing as the workforce changes over time. Transactional leadership, where leaders gain compliance and support by setting clear goals, offering rewards and providing assistance to achieve an expected level of performance, is no longer adequate. Today, we need to be more transformational as leaders, which means inspiring others and rising above our own personal needs in the interest of a common cause.

Transformational leaders are authentic and genuine, able to provide a clear vision of the future and motivate others to join them, especially in times of growth, change and crisis. Employees are seeking a two-way relationship with leaders where they are accepted as adult human beings in the workplace. They want leaders who understand that they are self-motivated to succeed, so need to feel valued, trusted, listened to, appreciated and like they belong.

Research by Dale Carnegie shows that the top three drivers of employee engagement are trust in leadership, pride in an organisation and connectedness with an immediate manager.[31] Gallup reports that managers account for up to 70% of the variance in employee engagement scores.[32] Leadership is such an important component for creating a great workplace, but it can be difficult to gain consistency across how managers treat their teams. A document detailing the company purpose and values is a great place to start to set the expectations for the organisation, but with leadership being so important, we need to take it one step further.

Leadership charter

One way to set the expectations of leadership in your organisation is to have a leadership charter. This details the ground rules and what you expect from leaders within the organisation.

To create your charter, bring your leadership group together and discuss what makes a good leader in general. Who epitomises good leadership among people you know, have worked with or admire? From that, determine the kind of qualities and behaviours the group wants leaders in your organisation to have, and then list them out.

Next, as a group, take that (probably lengthy) list and cut it down to maybe five to eight things, behaviours and qualities that you want to define 'what leadership looks like at our organisation'. For example, 'We want to have fun and open communication, be as transparent as possible, listen and empathise'. That will become the leadership charter.

As an individual, take the behaviours in the charter and commit to how you are going to demonstrate them over the next quarter. Let's say the behaviour is 'We have fun'. You can commit to demonstrating this by setting up a Slack channel with a theme every week for photos team members can share. This week's theme may be 'crazy hats', next week 'animals I have seen on my walk', the week after 'things that are blue' and so forth.

The table shows an example of ways to commit to the things, behaviours and qualities set out in the charter:

What leadership looks like	What I commit to do
Provide a plan and a vision	Quarterly all-employee update
	Frame meetings with the 'why'
Engage and inspire	Walk the floor and have a chat with two to three team members every day
Encourage personal growth	Encourage others to gain external mentors and bring development ideas to team meetings
Give and receive feedback	Provide timely feedback and actively seek it in one-to-ones and via a 360
Have fun	Set up a Slack channel with a weekly theme so the team can post photos

The left-hand column of this table is the leadership charter, which is made available throughout the business, for example on the intranet, in the employee handbook and employee benefits book, and displayed on the walls beside the values. Each quarter, the leadership group members discuss the right-hand column with each other and their teams to keep them accountable and identify if any changes need to be made.

One-to-ones

Leadership today is about understanding your employees not just as employees, but as people. This enables your employees to bring their 'whole selves to work'. The first step is to understand your team members.

This is not a new concept in business. Back in 1927, the Hawthorne plant of the Western Electric Company spent five years studying thousands of workers to determine how different changes to their workplace would impact productivity.[33] The researchers made changes to the lighting, rest periods, coffee breaks and even methods of payment. They offered employees free lunch, shorter workdays and weeks, different locations, overtime and financial incentives, but what the study found was that when the workers were given special attention, their productivity increased, regardless of what changes were made in the work setting. This phenomenon has become known as the 'Hawthorne Effect' and remains a foundation of organisational psychology.

One of the easiest ways for you as a leader to show special attention to your employees is to have regularly scheduled one-to-ones with them. As part of this one-to-one, always ask questions around how they are thinking and feeling. For example:

- If you were given a million dollars to do another job, what would it be?
- Is there anything right now that is worrying you?
- If you ran this company, what is the first thing you would change?

If your one-to-one focuses solely on daily work and operational issues, then you'll never get to fully understand your employees and what is driving and motivating them. It is in these consistent one-to-ones that you will build trust with your team members, help to increase engagement and discover early any problems that you can then work on together. This is why regular structured performance reviews are also important, but more on that soon.

The focus of one-to-ones is for the leader to listen. Active listening is where you try to understand the other person's viewpoint, which means not just hearing the words, but listening for meaning in what they're saying.

To become a better listener:

- Make a decision to listen and give the person your undivided attention.

- Put away your phone, turn off notifications on your computer and focus.
- Do not interrupt. Make notes if you want to come back to a point later.
- Keep eye contact.
- Ask open questions.

While you are speaking, you aren't listening. The more you listen, the more others will share.

CASE STUDY: WHY AREN'T THEY ENGAGED?

I knew a great leader who'd owned a business for many years, but she was having difficulties. She wasn't feeling like her senior management team members were on board and engaged, and some high performers had resigned unexpectedly within the last year.

When I asked her about what motivated her direct reports and their career ambitions, she realised she didn't know. Although she had regular team meetings and one-to-ones with them, she had never asked these types of questions.

It can feel awkward to suddenly 'turn on' that switch, so I advised her to be up front with her direct reports and let them know she had a coach who'd suggested that she needed to understand more about her team, and the first part of that was to understand their career goals and what excited them about work. Then she would be able to support them better. I gave her the questions we looked at earlier to help start those conversations.

She was surprised to discover that she'd assumed everyone was motivated by the same things that she was. Of course, that wasn't the case at all, but she now had the information available on how to motivate and engage her team individually. She kept adding other coaching questions to her one-to-one meetings to continue to understand her direct reports more, and over time these types of questions become 'normal'. This helped her not just to build trust and loyalty, but also to keep a finger on the pulse of what was happening with the team as individuals.

Leadership development

Too frequently, business owners/CEOs promote people into leadership roles because of their subject matter expertise without first teaching them the mindset and skills required to lead. From the talent matrix process of your development plans, you will have identified those who have the potential and the desire to develop as leaders in your business. Now you need to focus on areas of development for your current and emerging leaders.

There are hundreds of thousands of leadership books and probably as many courses out there, so choosing what to focus on for development can be overwhelming. Two great places to start are with growth mindset and positive intent.

Growth mindset

Having a growth mindset is based on the research of Dr Carol Dweck.[34] It is about believing that everyone can learn and develop and achieve, assuming that skills and talents are built and can grow, effort leads to personal growth, challenges are an opportunity, mistakes are a chance to learn, and feedback is useful and appreciated.

Subsequent research by Dweck and her colleagues into growth mindset in organisations found that employees who are in a more fixed mindset (the opposite of growth mindset) organisation worry about failing, so are less likely to be innovative.[35] They regularly keep secrets and take shortcuts to get ahead, whereas employees in growth mindset organisations are considered by their leaders to be more innovative, collaborative and committed to learning and growth, and to have more potential.

When leaders have a growth mindset, they see opportunities rather than challenges and actively grow their team members. These same leaders will seek feedback and create a culture of trust and accountability.

Positive intent

To assume positive intent means to choose to believe the best of people and trust that they have good intentions. It includes the idea that we all have good reason for what we are saying and doing while accepting that not everyone is like us.

When you think something is a problem, is this due to your perspective or is it a genuine issue? If you assume positive intent, you avoid making negative assumptions and statements and focus first on understanding. This makes it easier to have productive conversations with your team members and work together with them within a two-way relationship.

CASE STUDY: POSITIVE INTENT AT WORK

Lachy Gray, the co-founder of Yarno, and I discussed positive intent and how he uses this mindset in his business.[36] During this podcast episode, he said:

'Giving and receiving feedback is fundamental, because there will be things that we (my employees and I) need to speak up about. We will need to give each other feedback. We will need to have difficult conversations. If we're neither encouraged to do that nor trained in how to do it, it's highly unlikely that we will a) do it or b) do it well.

'Part of giving feedback is assuming positive intent. If you do something in the workplace, for example, that really frustrates me, I change my lens on that and say, "If I assume positive intent, perhaps Karen didn't do that intentionally. She doesn't know what the impact of that behaviour is on me, so there's an opportunity for me to share that impact with her so we can align going forward."

'What my teams and I have found is that regularly receiving and giving positive feedback feels good. We need to do it, so that when the time comes to have a difficult conversation, there is some level of trust there. If I'm giving you constructive feedback and you assume positive intent on my side, then you frame the feedback as an attempt to help rather than a put down for the sake of my career or my next promotion.'

Use focus areas such as growth mindset and positive intent, along with your leadership charter, to guide the development for those employees with potential as leaders. This will equip them with the expectations and mindset they require to lead others effectively before they even begin managing people.

Managing performance

It is not uncommon for me to have a conversation with a manager who tells me that their team members aren't performing. For example, 'I have a salesperson who isn't selling' is something I hear regularly, but when I ask how the employee is tracking against targets, I discover either they don't have any targets at all or the targets aren't clear and trackable.

If someone hasn't been given a performance standard to meet, it is impossible for them to know what great looks like, and just as difficult for you to manage. The more you and your reports fail to measure performance, the more demotivated employees can become. Firstly, the individual doesn't feel rewarded for their efforts, and secondly, they feel a sense of injustice and frustration when colleagues seem to be 'getting away with it' or their own lack of productivity becomes a barrier for their success.

Goal setting is something that business leaders often either miss, do poorly or complete quickly simply to tick a box. As humans, we all have an innate need for competence, autonomy and achievement. Giving your employees input into their work and together setting the common understanding of behaviours that you want as a team meets this psychological need and encourages engagement, which drives performance.

Often, the goal setting process is wrapped into the dreaded annual performance review. Why dreaded? Because in my experience, the vast majority of people – managers, employees and HR teams alike – actively dislike annual performance reviews. They have become a forced administrative exercise completed once per year, and people often feel judged and demotivated as a result of the review. It is not surprising that large corporations such as GE[37], Adobe[38], Gap[39], Deloitte[40], Accenture[41], Microsoft and Dell[42] have all been reported to have removed the traditional annual performance review.

Before you consider removing the whole process, though, know that even the organisations that no longer use the annual performance review process have put something in its place. The reality is that without a formal process, many managers won't give employees feedback and may not think to talk to them about development or set goals. For most employees, a formal conversation to discuss how they are performing, the need for changes to their workload and development makes them feel listened to and valued, which is one of the keys to engagement.

CASE STUDY: THE IMPORTANCE OF STRUCTURED FEEDBACK

I worked with a business owner who had a large span of control. She did not have managers between her and her twenty-five employees, so she had a lot on her plate. Although there was an open-door policy within her business and anyone could go and speak to her at any time, there was no proactive approach to feedback as she believed she didn't have time for this.

This resulted in new employees being unsure if they were doing a good job or not. They felt lost and confused about how they fitted into the organisation. Many left within their first few months because they couldn't get the development they needed to get up to speed as there was no one available to support them proactively in their new role.

Existing employees would also leave for career development opportunities as they didn't see a career path for them within the organisation, although potentially, one could have been made.

Unfortunately, once someone has psychologically made the decision to leave, it is often too late to change their mind. This is why it is so important to have proactive scheduled meetings with your team members to uncover what is happening in their day-to-day work along with their worries, fears, hopes and aspirations.

Performance reviews

A successful performance review process is one which is:

- Based on having a valuable conversation and not filling out a form
- Held at least quarterly
- Future focused

Many performance review processes aren't effective as they become a 'tick and flick' exercise. Companies use Word documents, Google forms or perhaps a software program to report on compliance and force the completion of forms, but this is missing the whole point. For a performance review to have value, it needs to be all about the conversation between the leader and the employee.

The organisations that have moved away from the traditional performance review have other processes in its place. Some rely on technology to enable teams to provide continuous feedback. Others simply allocate four times in the year where managers and their reports have a guided conversation. The biggest change when you're moving from a traditional performance review process to one of meaningful discussions between employees and their managers is that the manager's role becomes coach rather than evaluative judge.

Here are six steps to move to a more collaborative conversational approach to performance reviews:

1. Determine the why

The first thing to determine is why your current review process isn't working. Have you received employee feedback that it is not a good use of time? Do you have evidence that reviews aren't being completed? Are employees completing development plans? What are your engagement survey results telling you?

Then ask yourself why you are wanting to change. Why do you think it is important to have a structured review process? Determining your why will enable you to focus on what your new process looks like. Before going too far, you need to take your own thinking on why the review process isn't working and chat about it with your teams.

2. Consult

Ask your team members what they find works or doesn't work with the current process. Be honest about why you think it isn't working.

Ask them what it is that they want. Having done this with many focus groups, I can almost guarantee you their replies will be along the lines of:

- Open conversations
- Two-way feedback
- To know I'm doing a good job
- Recognition
- Development
- Frequent feedback (monthly or quarterly)

3. Refine

Take all this information and refine it. You'll probably find that the new process will include structured conversations rather than completing forms; discussions that are future focused rather than scores that rate past performance; and managers needing to listen and coach rather than evaluate and judge. If your business currently ties pay rises to performance reviews, you may also need to determine your new remuneration strategy.

4. Pilot

This is a big change and for some the shift will create anxiety. It is also an all-company change, so if you have more than forty staff, a pilot will help to iron out any kinks before you go into full launch mode.

It is best to pick one or two small teams in different areas of the business for the pilot. Ask them to try the process and report back before you launch. Their (hopefully positive) feedback will be helpful to 'sell' the new process to the rest of the teams.

5. Train

Managers and employees will need help to adjust. Use online videos, written instructions and/or face-to-face workshops to explain the differences between the traditional process and your new one. Incorporate focused training for leaders on coaching and communication techniques.

6. Evaluate

Continuous evaluation of your new process is key to keeping it useful and valued. What works today may not work in two years' time. As performance discussions are one of the keys to employee engagement, it is worth the time and effort to continually review and improve them.

Goal setting

The first step to managing performance and holding proactive performance reviews is setting goals. Research completed by Locke and Latham has given us our modern understanding of goal setting.[43] Not only do their studies show that there is a link between goal setting and performance in the workplace, but they also published five principles to consider when we're goal setting. Here's a brief summary of those principles:

- **Commitment** – this is how attached we are to the goal and our resolve to achieve it. We are more likely to give up when we are less committed to goals, particularly more challenging goals. Where there is strong commitment, there is a significant association between goals and performance.

- **Clarity** – when a goal is vague, it can be difficult for someone to understand, and is less motivating. For example, telling someone to try hard or do their best is less effective than saying, 'Try to get more than eighty sales this week'. Goals are motivating when they are clear and can be measured.

- **Challenge** – we are motivated by achieving, and anticipating the achievement, of challenging but attainable goals. Challenging goals can improve performance through feelings of confidence and satisfaction, whereas goals that are not attainable lead to dissatisfaction and frustration.

- **Complexity** – complex goals can become overwhelming and negatively impact morale, productivity and motivation. If the task is too complex for their skill level, even the highly motivated employees can become disillusioned.

- **Feedback** – goal setting is more effective when there is clear and immediate feedback, which ensures that we can take action if the employee's performance falls below the standard required to achieve a goal. Feedback also allows employees to reflect and set new more attainable and challenging goals.

For goal setting, you may have come across the acronym SMART, which stands for specific, measurable, attainable, relevant and time-bound. This nicely fits with the goal setting principles.

The performance review process can provide a great framework for setting goals at the start of the year, but before setting individual goals, make sure you have some overarching company goals. If you don't, do a quick balanced scorecard exercise with your team where you identify what goals and KPIs (which are the measures of the goals) would enable your business to be successful this year from a financial, operations, customer and people perspective.

Common KPIs are:

- Financial – revenue, costs, profit

- Operations – may be the number of widgets created each month or an efficiency program to create a certain value of savings
- Customer – net promoter score (NPS)[44] and retention percentage
- People – employee turnover percentage and engagement survey scores

When you present the overarching goals and KPIs to employees, ask them to choose three to five goals for their role that align with the company goals. For example, Isaac is an events coordinator and the company goal is to increase the customer base through retention and new business. The KPI for that goal is a NPS of sixty-two or higher. His personal goal is to develop a step-by-step process for a new product launch event.

In a SMART framework, it could look something like this:

S Specific goal	M Success measured by	A How is it attainable?	R Is it realistic?	T Timeframe
Develop step-by-step process for a new product launch event	Process shared and implemented for next event. Feedback sought from stakeholders	Time allocated each Friday to complete	✓	By 30 March

Once an employee has set their goals, then their manager checks these and agrees that they are the most important for the employees' role this year and they are SMART. The manager and employee also need to consider if the goals are challenging. If the goals are tied to incentives, people tend to be more cautious with setting them, which reduces the challenge and therefore the motivating power of goal setting. Empowering employees to set their own goals helps with commitment but be aware that if an employee is new to the organisation or the goal setting process, they may need your help to come up with that initial draft.

Once the goals are meeting the principles of commitment, clarity, challenge and complexity, you need to consider feedback. This is why the frequency of performance reviews is so important. If goals are set at the start of the year and a formal meeting is held every quarter to review progress in the goals and employee-development plans, is that enough?

Depending on the goals, it may be, but don't hold on to feedback until the review. Make providing and asking for feedback a regular continuous process. It not only builds trust, it means that there are never any surprises. Employees hear on a regular basis if they are doing great work or if there are areas for improvement, which is motivating and reduces the anxiety many people feel before attending a formal performance review meeting.

A quick checklist for feedback:

- **Balanced.** Check that your feedback gives a balanced view. Only giving positive comments can be as unhelpful as all negative.
- **Relevant.** Keep it to what matters, ie what the employee has control over.
- **Specific.** Avoid general statements when you deliver feedback, such as, 'You are *always* late with that report'. Is it really always late? If not, how often is it late?
- **Tailored.** For example, having a team meeting to remind everyone to do XYZ will not be as effective as discussing it directly with the employee who is currently not doing XYZ.
- **Follow up.** Providing feedback is about improving performance and developing the employee, so let the employee know whether you have seen positive change or not.

When it comes to changing the way you do performance reviews, I recommend you rename them completely. This sets the expectation that what you do in your business is not the disliked annual review. Calling them 'quarterly feedback sessions' or 'quarterly check-ins', for example, can help set the tone from the start.

Communicate, communicate, communicate

The key with communication is that you need to communicate, communicate, and then communicate. The first time you announce something, send an email or post a video, not everyone is going to listen intently or understand what it means for them.

One thing communication is *not* is leaders speaking at employees, but not allowing time and space to listen. According to Gallup, employees whose managers hold regular meetings with them are nearly three times more engaged than those with managers who don't.[45] Officevibe reported that 43% of highly engaged employees receive feedback at least once a week, and while 65% of employees want more feedback, 58% of managers think they already give enough.[46]

I have found communication is usually one of the lowest scoring areas when I'm conducting engagement surveys for clients. Lack of clear communication is also one of the most common complaints by employees regarding their manager. Interestingly, this is often received by the leadership team with exasperation as they don't understand how they could communicate more.

As your business gets larger, it becomes more difficult for you to have open communication and cross collaboration, and to prevent silos. The reality is that the

GROW

more people you have in your organisation, the more communication lines you have and the more complicated communication becomes.

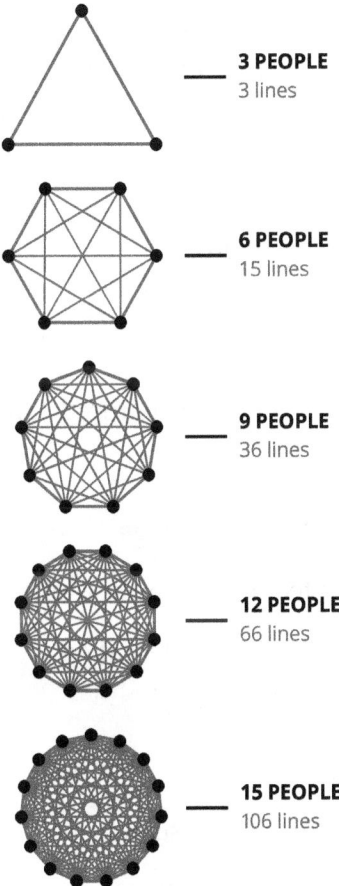

As this image shows, with three people in your organisation, there are an easy three lines of communication. Moving to four, five or six people, you are already introducing additional lines and the complexity begins. Once you are at fifteen people, there are 106 possible lines of communication.

This is why you need to be really clear about how and when you are communicating. The best way to do this is to have an internal communications plan, and it doesn't need to be complicated or resource intensive to put this together.

Communications plan

At the start of the year, map out the communication milestones. These are the events, projects or activities that include structured communication, for example:

- Quarterly all-staff meetings
- Half-yearly team planning sessions
- End of financial year celebration
- Monthly team meetings
- Manager one-to-ones
- New starter induction session
- Lunch and learn workshops
- Employee round tables

Once you have the list of all the structured communication activities, put them into a table, where each activity is in a separate column. Then in a row underneath, put the frequency. This could be monthly or quarterly, or it could be specific months/dates in the year.

The next row is the objectives of the activity. What is the purpose? What do you want to achieve? Consider the key messages – what are the takeaways you want from the audience? Who is the audience, how will you communicate and who is accountable (delivering the message) and responsible for organising the communication activity?

That is your first communication activity, ie your first time communicating the message. An example of this table is on the following pages.

Next you need to consider Communicate2, how you remind everyone, and Communicate3 is confirming the message.

Let's look at quarterly all-employee team meetings as an example. You put in the dates and the objectives, which will be the same for each meeting; what may change are the key messages.

Internal communications plan

Activity: What is the event, project, process, activity?	Quarterly all-employee team meeting	Monthly team meetings
Communicate 1		
Frequency and/or dates	March, June, September, December	Monthly
Objective: What do you want to achieve?	• Update on company progress to goals (revenue, new business, key metrics) • Keep employees informed	• Discuss current work in progress, roadblocks and any outstanding actions • Team socialisation • Keep team members informed
Who is the target audience?	All employees	All employees in their own teams
What are the three to five key messages?	• eg Revenue has increased 15% thanks to great efforts across the teams • Onboarded three new customers last month • Lost XYZ customer due to ABC	
Method: How will you communicate?	• Verbal • Use dot point • PowerPoint slides • Record any questions	• Verbal • May have a written agenda • Keep meeting minutes
Accountable: Who is delivering the communication?	MD	Team managers
Responsible: Who is organising the communication activity?	Office manager	Team managers

Monthly/fortnightly/ weekly one-to-ones	New employee starts	Twice per year employee round tables
Frequency agreed between manager and employee (at a minimum monthly)		April, October
Engage and motivate team members through listening and offering support one-to-one	• Engage and inspire new team members • Helps set culture and behavioural expectations	• Employees have an open conversation with a senior manager who is not their direct manager • Enables relationships to be developed cross functionally, builds engagement, gives senior management an insight into those they may not usually interact with
All employees individually	New starters	All employees randomly selected into small groups
	Purpose of organisation and values	• We are here to listen to your feedback, suggestions and ideas • We are interested in everyone as an individual
Verbal	Verbal	Verbal, but take notes
Team managers	MD	Senior management
Team managers	Office manager	Office manager

Internal communications plan

Activity: What is the event, project, process, activity?	Quarterly all-employee team meeting	Monthly team meetings
Communicate 2		
Remind	Email – information included in monthly staff newsletter	Email – send minutes of meeting
Communicate 3		
Confirm	Progress to goals updated on intranet/noticeboards	One-to-ones with team members

For example, this quarter, you may want to talk about the fact that revenue has increased thanks to the great efforts across the teams and celebrate onboarding three new customers in the last month, but you also have to talk about how the business lost XYZ customer due to ABC. Because the key messages will change every quarter, although you are setting up the plan at the start of the year, you need to refer to it each quarter and update it for the next quarterly meeting. In terms of the person responsible, it may be that this is the person doing the communication, but you may also list anyone assisting with the meeting.

The next decision is how to communicate the key message. Is it verbal, or will you be using dot points on a PowerPoint slide? Will it be face-to-face or using Zoom? Are you recording the meetings? Are you

Monthly/fortnightly/weekly one-to-ones	New employee starts	Twice per year employee round tables
• Verbal thank you • Reiterate key takeaways/ actions from meeting	Follow-up thank-you email	Follow-up thank-you email
Email – follow up key takeaways from meeting	New starters mentioned in quarterly team meetings	Update in two quarterly meetings regarding feedback received and actions taken

taking a record of any questions? Are you asking for questions before the meeting?

Communicate1 might be an all-staff Zoom meeting. Then Communicate2 could be an email staff newsletter with the key points that were covered in the meeting and Communicate3 is publishing your progress to goals on the intranet and noticeboard as they are the key objectives to that communication.

This is a simple communications framework. The important part is to think about the main communication events throughout the year and plan the communication up front. As you can see in the example, the key messages for the monthly team meetings and one-to-ones haven't been completed because they will change with each meeting, and with each team and individual employee. You do need to consider them prior to each of those meetings, though.

Reducing silos

Sharing goals and accountabilities

It is important to have a mechanism for sharing goals across the business to improve cross communication. Each year, when you are setting the goals for the business, cascade them through the managers and the team members. The next step is to share team and individual goals across the organisation. Missing this step can cause silos and miscommunication as goals may not be aligned across the teams, even if they are aligned to the business.

For example, say I am the marketing manager and the company goal is to achieve $X revenue. I share my individual goals with my peers, and I share my team goals with the other teams.

As I'm doing this, the sales manager realises that although their team has the same company goal of $X revenue, their team goals don't align with my marketing team goals. The marketing team has a plan to focus on social media over the next three-quarters and forecasts an increase of Y% in leads, whereas the sales team has a plan to focus on retention of existing customers and upselling those customers to achieve their revenue targets. They will not have the capacity to manage an increase in new leads and onboarding of new customers.

This is why it is important to make sure goals are aligned, otherwise over the year, there will be tensions and potentially conflict between teams. Each will feel the other teams are not helping to achieve either their or the company goals.

Social opportunities

Another way to reduce silos is for different teams to get to know each other. As human beings, we are sociable creatures; even those of us who are introverts still want to know, like and trust other people.

Find opportunities for everybody to get together. Some organisations use social committees; these are great, but the members often get busy in their own work and tired of organising events for everyone else, or people leave the organisation and new starters don't join the committee.

If there isn't a social committee, it tends to land on one person in the organisation who happens to put up their hand to organise social opportunities. Alternatively, the office manager or assistant is nominated simply because of their role. Over time, they find that they don't always have the support of other employees and feel like they're chasing everybody. As a result, they become disillusioned and stop organising activities.

A better way to keep social activities happening is to have them run by employee groups rather than a set committee. Split the organisation into social teams and give each team a budget and some guidelines around the types and frequency of the activities they are responsible for organising.

I have a client with three senior managers. My client split the employees into three cross-functional groups and each manager took a group for their social team. Each group has a name, and its members are responsible for creating one social activity every quarter, so the business leaders can communicate that this quarter, X event is brought to you by the ABC team. This brings a sense of ownership to the employees, along with a bit of competition over which group can organise the best event. Above all, it's a fun opportunity for all employees to collaborate and get to know each other.

Language

A third way to reduce silos and improve cross communication is to consider the language that your managers are using to talk about other teams. It can be easy to slip into an 'us versus them' mindset – a sure-fire way to start silos.

The psychological terms 'in groups' and 'out groups' describe favouritism among social groups.[47] As human beings, we are fallible and tend to identify with our 'in group'. In a business context, this may be our own team members, and they are who we look to protect. The 'out group' may be members of another team, and we don't identify with them so we don't protect them; we may even seek to do them harm.

During the COVID-19 pandemic, I noticed Australians moved away from talking about themselves as Australians and instead talked about themselves from the perspective of the state or territory they live in. The State premiers were openly judging each other in press conferences, accusing each other of taking too many vaccines, keeping borders closed for too long or not going into lockdown fast enough.

In the workplace, we need to be aware of this tendency and not use the kind of language that can instil the idea that other teams are the 'out group'. Having goals and accountabilities shared across the business will help, so will the communications plan, but as leaders, we have a role to be aware and intentional with our language.

Let's say that I have a particular project and there's another manager who I feel is a barrier to me completing that project. If I say to my team that the reason we can't do this is because that person is doing X, that's a really quick and easy way to start a silo and facilitate the idea of us versus them.

One of the best ways to agree on language in the organisation is to implement a team charter alongside the leadership charter, depending on the size and type of business you have. This helps to reduce silos because everyone in the business is agreeing as a team what behaviours are acceptable and what each individual is going to do to demonstrate those behaviours. Then when there are conflicting situations, you can refer back to your company values and your leadership or team charter, using these to take a step back and work through conflicting priorities. You and your teams can then express yourselves in ways that show you are all in this together and can find a solution.

Creating a team charter is a similar process to creating a leadership charter, but you start with the question 'What makes a great team?' Google has some resources on rework.withgoogle.com on what makes effective teams. Use these and your team members' own experiences to come up with a long list of qualities and behaviours, and then work as a team to reduce this to a list of five to eight which demonstrate how you want to work together. The team charter can be refined and finalised, and then shared with other teams to help reduce silos and improve cross communication.

Summary

We are two-thirds of the way through the Find, Grow, Keep methodology. Having successfully hired and onboarded great people, you now know the HR practices to grow them within your business. You are consistently focusing on leadership, performance, goal setting, feedback, developing others and effective communication.

Next, you need to ensure you have the right processes and practices in place to keep great people for as long as possible so your business can grow and thrive.

5
Keep

Once you have found great employees and are growing them with the business, the question turns to how to keep these people. Whereas our parents or grandparents lived in a time when people had one job for decades, the national average for tenure in a job is now just over three years.[48]

Having a structured framework for listening to your people, providing career paths and recognising and rewarding great performance and behaviours will create the platform to keep your workplace relevant and engaging. Great employees will feel valued, which leads to them being engaged and productive, and the longer this continues, the more successful your business will be.

Listening

As we saw in the last chapter, a common complaint from employees is lack of communication. This complaint is heard across businesses of different sizes and industries and is often a source of frustration for business owners and leaders. They point to a litany of in-house communications and ask, 'What else can we possibly do?'

What I find employees are actually saying is that they are not *listened* to enough. Communication is vitally important and will help you grow your people, but it is the act of listening that will keep them.

The most effective listening mechanisms I have found are:

- Exit surveys/interviews for departing employees
- First-impression surveys for new starters
- Yearly engagement and satisfaction survey for all employees
- Founder/CEO round tables

Exit surveys/interviews

Sometimes I am asked if exit interviews are worthwhile. Particularly if the employer doesn't regret the fact a certain employee has resigned, why would they even try to find out more about their reasons for leaving?

Any information employees can give about their experience at your workplace is worthwhile, but it is important to consider the type of information that will be most valuable and the best method to get that information. Sometimes exit interviews – where an employee discusses their reasons for leaving and employee experience with another individual (usually a member of the HR team) – can result in an exhausting meeting and pages of notes that are difficult to quantify or action. Was this just that one person's experience? How do you know if the problem is broader? What if this was an under-performing employee – how reliable is their feedback?

I recommend building a survey into an online platform for the employee to complete, and then providing them with the option to have a follow-up discussion if they would like it. This enables you to standardise questions and answers. Over time, when multiple people have completed the survey, you can look for trends.

CASE STUDY: THE VALUE OF A DEPARTING EMPLOYEE SURVEY

A client with around seventy employees has an employee turnover rate of 20%. That means on average, just over one person leaves per month. As soon as they receive a resignation or make a role redundant, the client sends the departing employee a link to an online survey, but also asks them if they would like to have a face-to-face or telephone discussion. Towards the end of the survey, they are asked if they would like to discuss more with HR, and if so to leave their contact details.

Using this method, the client gets a much higher response rate (many people are too busy or not interested in an interview, but will fill in the survey), receiving quantifiable data that they can collate and share with the senior team each quarter or half-year, depending on the amount of data. This information provides important trends which the client can use as part of the broader picture of listening to their employees.

Designing the survey is important, so I recommend you take the time to think about the information that will be useful to you. Asking questions around why the employee made the decision to leave and how satisfied they were across areas of employee experience are important, but so are questions around if they have ever experienced or witnessed bullying, harassment and discrimination.

Design the questions with multiple-choice or drop-down responses the employee can select from. This will make the data easier to compare later. Include lots of opportunities for comments or open text so they can provide any additional information which may be relevant.

First-impression surveys

Send this survey to a new employee at around the three-month stage. As its name suggests, it is designed to capture the first impressions the employee has had of your organisation.

The best place to start is to use an online survey platform and create a version of your exit survey with different wording, so rather than 'Please select the reasons you are leaving XYZ Company', you would say 'Please select the reasons why you decided to join XYZ Company'. This immediately gives you additional comparison information, so when you collate results quarterly or half-yearly, you're not only looking at trends for exiting and starting employees, you can compare across the groups.

For example, a client's departing employees were citing wanting growth and development along with the chance to further their career as key reasons for their decision to resign. Looking at the first-impressions data, the client could see these same two items as key reasons for people joining. This gave them a clear signal that the company needed to do more to proactively develop employees and demonstrate career paths in the organisation.

The first-impression survey needs to contain some questions that are not in the exit survey. Ideally, these will come from your yearly engagement and satisfaction survey so that you can get a sense of whether areas of focus are translating for new employees. This is the perfect time to understand if the onboarding process is effective and ask new employees for their ideas on what could make the workplace better.

Yearly engagement and satisfaction survey

Imagine you have employees who are focused and attentive to their work and believe in the organisation's purpose. They don't just 'get things done'; they go above and beyond, achieving goals and being willing to do more. They put forward ideas, collaborate, take minimal time off, attract and retain customers and increase your profits.

Sound good?

That is the essence of engagement, which is why so many organisations want to increase their engagement levels. The only way to know your business's level of engagement is to measure it, and that is where engagement surveys become so valuable.

Employee engagement is different to job satisfaction, but they are related. Employees are naturally going to have higher job satisfaction if they're engaged, but job satisfaction is about being fulfilled in their work rather than the psychological state of being engaged, which is more related to motivation.

We have already touched on employee experience. The simplest way to think about it is that it describes everything an employee experiences within the workplace during the employment lifecycle, from how they are recruited to how they are led and developed, the physical workplace, the technology they've used and how they eventually depart. This includes their feelings as well as the experiences, so engagement is essentially the output of their employee experience.

Although many business leaders run employee satisfaction and engagement surveys, once they have the survey results, they often don't do much with the information other than referencing the scores in various reports. If you're only focusing on measuring engagement, you're not focusing on increasing engagement, which means not a lot is going to change. In fact, you're likely to decrease engagement as your employees become demotivated and disillusioned about engagement surveys when they don't see any changes happen as a result.

I recommend you conduct an engagement and satisfaction survey yearly as this gives you a baseline to measure your workplace culture over time. You can use an external organisation to run a survey, or you can create your own. Either way, ensure the questions make sense for your organisation and your employees feel safe in answering them.

Consider how to ensure the survey responses will be anonymous and confidential. This will enable you to receive truthful responses and a higher level of participation. One of the reasons my clients use my business to do their surveys is to ensure the data is secured on our servers. My team can assure respondents that they will be anonymous as only the de-identified results are collated and provided to their managers.

Align questions to engagement and satisfaction, as well as to your organisation's values, the purpose of your organisation and its strategy and goals. What are you looking to do over the next three to five years?

If you're looking to implement new products or services, then some of your questions may be around innovation. Ask your employees how easy it is to put ideas forward. If your business is looking at merging with other companies, then you want to be able to develop and retain top talent, so you may be asking questions regarding training and development and if employees feel they have a career path with the organisation. Looking at your questions through a strategic lens that's specific to your company is going to give you the most value.

Questions that measure employee engagement are those around putting in extra effort, recommending family or friends to work for your company, having a sense of belonging and believing in the purpose of the organisation. Questions around organisation and

KEEP

job satisfaction will give you important information about your employee experience. These are questions about how effective training and development are, if employees have regular one-to-ones with their manager and what internal communication is like.

Once the survey is complete, collate the data and look at it critically. If you are getting high scores in certain areas, that is a fantastic thing to leverage in your business, internally and externally. For example, if you get great scores for development opportunities, make that part of your employer brand. That is what you sell in the marketplace when you're looking for candidates as it helps you to get great employees on board. If you're getting low scores in development and you know that that's a critical component of what your organisation needs, then that's clearly an area you need to focus on.

Depending on the size of your organisation and the results of the survey, you may have focus groups with your employees to gain more understanding as to the context of the scores. Employee surveys contain standard questions and people are going to rate them differently and through different lenses, so there can be fantastic value in having focus groups where you discuss the questions to get to the nuts and bolts of what you can do to increase employee engagement.

The most important and fun part of this process is the action planning. The action plan sits within your HR strategy rather than forming a separate plan. Because you have aligned your survey to your organisational goals and strategy up front, this should not be difficult to do.

As you put together actions as a result of the survey, consult with key staff members and leaders to create some buy-in. Once the strategy is completed, share it with your organisation and track its progress as you would for other core business goals.

Running a survey once per year gives enormous value, but it's just a point-in-time view, so run a smaller survey, sometimes called a 'pulse check', every few months around key questions. If you have a larger organisation, run short surveys (around ten questions) with a random selection of employees each month. This will give you ongoing feedback and help you keep 'on the pulse' with what is happening in your organisation.

Founder/CEO round tables

One of the great benefits of working for an SME is having direct access to the founder and/or senior team. This also benefits the senior team members as they can access and listen directly to different levels within the business.

As your business grows to more than forty employees, I recommend you implement round tables. This is where a random group of six to eight employees is invited to a meeting with a senior manager, who is not their direct manager, for an open and confidential discussion. The leader of the round table makes notes but doesn't tie the employee's name to the feedback so that employees can feel comfortable in sharing.

The leader facilitates the discussion with prepared questions, tailoring them to both the audience and specific concerns they may have around the workplace culture. They also include some standard questions that are asked at each session to help loosen up the group and gather information on consistent topics, for example:

- Why did you join our organisation and what keeps you here?
- Why do people leave?
- How do you describe the workplace culture here?
- Do you think we're focusing on the right things as a company?
- How do you feel senior leadership is doing?
- How am I doing? What can I do differently?

After each round table, the senior leader provides anonymised feedback to HR for review and to take any immediate action that may be required. If there is no HR in the business, then the round table leader takes responsibility for this. I recommend collating the feedback from each round table twice per year to identify any themes and help inform future HR strategy and initiatives.

Many years ago, I worked for a large multinational organisation which had a version of round table meetings called 'skip level meetings'. Each time a senior leader from head office came to Australia, they would hold meetings that would 'skip' levels so they could get feedback directly from employees two to three levels below them. Employees loved the opportunity to attend these meetings as it helped to build relationships and trust. On a broader level, it also helped to strengthen the open and collaborative workplace culture.

Career paths

As we discussed in Chapter 4, growth and development are important to employees and one of the top benefits they seek from employers. Career paths take that one step further and provide a pathway that enables your employees to see where development can take them.

Zig Ziglar is quoted as saying 'You don't build a business; you build people, and the people build the business'.[49] If you're not focusing on career development as a core offering to your employees, those who are driven will move on to another organisation.

Those who stay largely become people whose skills are stagnating, and they get disillusioned with the organisation. This reduces the productivity of the business as dysfunction creeps into the culture and a spiral of hiring, leaving, firing, hiring begins.

Although it is important for employees to own their career, it is equally important for you as the leader to support their career development and highlight how they can add to their career path through working in your business. In many cases, the career path won't be available within your business, but as you develop employees, they will become more efficient and take on more duties which will strengthen their skills and experience. This makes them the 'go to' person for other employees and this chain reaction helps create highly productive teams. The goal is to keep your employees engaged, and if they feel that their career is being developed, you can retain them for as long as possible.

Larger businesses may be able to structure clear career paths as X role has Y criteria to be met before the person can go to Z position. Even in these cases, though, employees can be frustrated with lack of development as it still requires Z position to be available. The benefit in organisations of under 100 employees is that you can personalise the career path, which not only shows the employee how much you value them, but also enables them to see progress over time, even if that isn't a brand-new position.

CASE STUDY: AMY'S CAREER CONVERSATION

Amy is identified through the talent matrix process as being high in potential and performance. Her manager discusses with Amy her career goals over the next one to three and five years.

Amy is currently a sales representative and she would like to be a sales director within five years. In this business, there is no sales director position as the owner wears that hat. Amy and her manager acknowledge this but discuss what other opportunities are available in the business over the next twelve months and make a plan using a long-term career goal template rather than the usual individual development plan.

Using this format, they discuss the annual goal that will help to build to the long-term career goal. Once they have agreed the annual goal, they explore which one goal for the quarter will help achieve that. To work towards that quarterly goal, what is the one thing Amy needs to do each month?

Long-term career goal – five years

Sales director

Medium-term career goal – two to three years

Managing a small team

Annual goal

To have opportunities to act in a supervisory position and understand more fully the skills and qualities needed to be successful as a sales manager and sales director.

Quarter 1

Discuss with at least two sales directors their career paths and what skills and qualities are important to be successful.

Monthly goals

Month 1	Reach out to sales directors on LinkedIn who show as 'open to mentoring' and set up meetings.	Done/ Not done ✓/✗
Month 2	Meet with one sales director and share what I learned from this meeting with my manager to help with my development.	Done/ Not done ✓/✗
Month 3	Meet with second sales director and share what I learned with my manager to help with my development.	Done/ Not done ✓/✗

Each quarter, Amy and her manager discuss, assess and set the next quarter's goal. Naturally, they are both busy people and there will be some months and quarters where they don't make a lot of progress. That is OK, provided that the discussions are still being held between Amy and her manager, so Amy feels that the organisation is interested in her career and is helping her to achieve her goals.

This process requires commitment and skill from the leader. If that is not available in the business, then it may be worth seeking an external coach who can assist with setting goals and keeping the employee on track.

Often, small businesses become extremely reliant on one employee. Perhaps they have the most technical knowledge about the products being offered or hold the main relationships with key clients, or they are responsible for the majority of sales. In these instances, the risk attached to the person leaving is so great that the business owner needs to review not just a career path, but a pathway to the employee buying into the business. Only take this option after great consideration and discussion with an accountant and lawyer, but it may be the best way to create stability and long-term profitability for the business.

Recognition

Recognition is a huge motivator. Research by the OC Tanner Institute shows that almost 80% of employees who quit their jobs say lack of appreciation was a key reason for leaving.[50] The study also found that in North America, 65% of employees had received no recognition or appreciation in the workplace in the last year.

The principles of recognition

Recognition is a fundamental human need. People who feel recognised at work contribute more to the workplace; in other words, they are more engaged. The key principles to recognition are to make it:

- Focused and specific
- Timely
- Differentiated
- Personal
- Larger purpose

Focused and specific

Employees need to understand exactly why they are being recognised. Focused and specific recognition not only makes them feel good, it also makes them more likely to do the same thing again in the future.

For example, just saying, 'Hey, you did a great job today' is not very motivating. Instead, try, 'In your presentation today, the way that you explained the statistics really brought our problem to life and helped us to understand the issue.' That is much more motivating.

Timely

You need to be recognising people at the time that they are doing great things; that's how you can make sure it sticks. If you tell me that something I did three months ago really helped you, it's nice, but it's not particularly motivational. Tell me at the time and it really gives me a lift.

Differentiated

Recognise different employees in different ways, and the same goes for different achievements. If you give everybody in the business the same sort of recognition no matter what they've done, it doesn't feel meaningful to them.

For example, maybe I did something that saved the company $10,000 while someone else did something that cost the company $10,000, but we both received the same recognition. Both things may have been great for the business in different ways, but as an employee, I find it difficult to feel that I've been recognised based on my particular achievement.

Personal

When I do workshops around recognition with employees, I ask people to tell me about their best experience of receiving recognition. Every single time, it is something really personal.

One person told me, 'I have a love of karate, and my manager went to my favourite supply store and bought me some equipment. It meant so much because she knew that is an activity I am passionate about; it was really personalised.'

Another said, 'My manager knew that I love a particular wine bar in the city, and he took the team there and bought me a bottle of amazing wine.'

Larger purpose

Tie recognition to the team and the larger purpose of the business. Make sure the achievement or behaviour you're recognising contributes to the story about what matters in the workplace. If I'm doing something that goes directly towards the goals of my workplace, that's more of a reason to recognise me than if I've decided on an idea that doesn't quite fit in.

Recognition frameworks

Many business owners have told me that they've tried recognition programs, but they haven't worked. For example, one of my clients paid for an expensive online platform which allowed people to recognise each other and award each other employee points. The employees could then use those points to purchase items from different stores, but my client was really frustrated when she spoke to me about the result.

'We paid all this money for this platform,' she told me, 'and then nobody used it.'

It's a common story. Online platforms have their place and there are some good ones out there, but the problem with recognition programs is that we humans have a negative bias. We are much more likely to notice things that are going badly than things that are going well. Another problem is that points systems don't always feel personal.

One of the frameworks that my team likes to recommend to people is called 'Appreciation at Work' by Gary Chapman and Paul White.[51] It's about recognising that not everybody likes to be appreciated in the same way, so Chapman and White have defined appreciation into five languages:

1. Words of affirmation
2. Quality time
3. Acts of service
4. Tangible gifts
5. Physical touch

Some leaders feel the need to recognise good work by giving money to their employees in the form of bonuses or vouchers. They are completely focused on financial gifts as the only meaningful way to recognise their employees, but the reality is they think this way because they personally value financial incentives. Maybe their employees don't.

I worked with somebody who really disliked public affirmation: this was her least preferred form of appreciation. If I stood up in a room and told everyone that she'd done a great job, it would make her feel sick and she would wish the floor would swallow her up. Instead, I would write my words of appreciation in a card and give it to her.

It's an important step to work out the way each employee prefers to be appreciated. Chapman and White have a tool for this on their website.[52] It's also important to develop a system that offers different levels of recognition. For example:

- **Shout outs.** Tell someone what you appreciated and why. You may do that in a public forum, if that's something they enjoy, or a one-to-one.

- **Small gifts.** This could be a simple card, branded chocolates or a company T-shirt.

- **Larger gifts.** These might be $50 to $100 in value, things like vouchers or fine wine. If employees are working remotely, it could be a voucher for a meal delivery service.

- **Team celebrations.** These can get up to a few hundred dollars: things like morning teas, Friday drinks, or taking the team out to lunch in someone's honour.

You can get organised around small gifts by using what I call the 'Recognition Rolodex'. This is a little box on your desk with a Rolodex of cards in it, each one saying something like 'Have a longer lunch today' or 'Take a day off'. These small things can be really meaningful. You can grab a card and give it to an employee immediately after they have completed the action you are praising, making it easy to provide timely recognition.

You can also make the reward personal. For example, if someone really likes coffee, choose a card that says 'Grab yourself a coffee on me'.

It's hard to make a program succeed without accountability, but how do you have that with a recognition program? One way is to ask every manager at your monthly meeting to describe who they have recognised this month and why. Every manager is accountable for recognising at least one person each month.

What happens over time is that managers know this question will come up in the meeting, so they look out for someone to recognise. In other words, they actively 'catch' someone doing something right. It's a great way to overcome the negative bias I mentioned earlier.

Another tip is to nominate someone in the organisation to have responsibility for monitoring the stock of small gifts. They check each month they are being used, and if not, they highlight that to you.

CASE STUDY: A RECOGNITION FRAMEWORK IN ACTION

One of my clients didn't have a recognition framework at all. When my team did their first staff engagement survey, only an average of 57% of employees agreed to the questions related to recognition (for example, 'My leader regularly gives me appropriate recognition').

My team created a recognition program based on the four levels we looked at earlier and implemented an accountability framework where the senior managers would discuss who they had given recognition to that month and why. Employees were empowered and encouraged to provide recognition to their colleagues by taking some small gifts from a common area or submitting a shout out for the monthly all-staff meeting.

After one year, the engagement score in the area of recognition increased to 70% and this trend continued. Three years later, that score was 88%.

It can be easy to fall into the trap of recognising only achievements, but it's also important to recognise how people are doing what they're doing. This is why many leaders tie their recognition programs to company values. Some use an online form for people to fill out when they are nominating someone for a higher level of recognition. This ensures that other employees know why that person is being recognised and how their behaviour links to the organisation's values.

This provides a moment of reflection and a safeguard against rewarding behaviour that may get results, but not in the right way. If you have someone who successfully completed a goal, but did it by being the proverbial bull in the china shop, then rewarding this achievement rewards the wrong behaviour. This can be really annoying and demotivating to other team members.

Rewards

Rewards in the workplace cover many things. There is the actual payment that employees receive in exchange for work; there are also bonuses or incentive schemes, commission payments and employee benefits.

Benefits are often non-monetary rewards such as workplace flexibility, volunteer days, birthday celebrations and access to personal and professional development. They can also be symbolic, such as role title, office size and access to other benefits. Ultimately, you want to reward your employees to increase their motivation.

Base pay/salary

Although we work to pay for our living expenses, there are many components that make up our overall satisfaction with our pay. These include not just our salary, but also how often we receive salary increases and how these are determined, how equitable we feel our salary is in comparison with other employees and what benefits we receive.[53]

My company has a free online quiz for business owners and leaders to complete to receive a benchmarked report on their organisation when it comes to workplace culture.[54] One of the questions asks whether the 'principles used to determine salaries and pay increases are documented and available to all employees'. Around three-quarters of responders indicate they do this 'only some of the time' or 'not at all'.

There is a huge opportunity here in a world of transparency around data, particularly if you consider that employees are expecting more transparency than ever before. In 2021, Apple employees started sharing their pay details with each other in an effort to understand pay equity.[55] Reportedly, the company kept trying to shut this down, including blocking related Slack channels. This of course created its own issues as Apple was then regarded as having something to hide.

Businesses need structured transparent documented processes for how they determine salaries and check for pay equity regularly. Where this occurs and the business leaders are comfortable in the methodology, it is likely to lead to higher employee satisfaction with pay.

The easiest way to do this is through a remuneration policy or statement within the employee handbook.

EXAMPLE: REMUNERATION POLICY

To support our company purpose and values, the key principles of our remuneration policy are to:

- Provide fair and equitable remuneration for employees across the organisation
- Attract and retain talented employees within the business
- Comply with workplace laws and regulations

This provides a structure whereby employees are paid fairly in line with the market for their position. Salary increases are provided to compensate for extra responsibilities where appropriate, otherwise on a yearly basis to compensate for inflation.

The actions that we take to achieve this strategy are as follows.

KEEP

Provide fair and equitable remuneration for employees across the organisation	Attract and retain talented employees within the business	Comply with workplace laws
1 All salaries are compared to market data to check that each individual is at or above the 60th percentile.	Before advertising a new position, market data is checked so that each individual is at or above the 60th percentile.	Apply increases where required following the Fair Work Commission annual wage review.
2 Salaries of employees in the same or similar positions are compared to check for equity. This includes checking the salary increase history of the employee.	Where an employee takes on additional responsibilities within their current role, the salary is reviewed against market data and comparable roles within the business.	Yearly salary increases for employees in line with customer price index.
3 Undertake pay gap analysis to identify and address any gender pay gaps.	When recruiting new employees, compare salary to be offered to those in comparable positions to check for any inconsistencies and gender pay bias.	
Annually	As occurs	Annually

Incentive schemes

Bonuses, incentive schemes and commission structures can have some differences, but for the purposes of this section, I will refer to monetary rewards beyond the base salary as an incentive scheme.

When people start getting paid for a task they already enjoy, they sometimes lose interest in it.[56] This paradox has been the subject of research for years and has important impacts on rewards in the workplace, including incentive schemes. To increase motivation, your incentive scheme must:

- Focus on the achievement of specific goals
- Be perceived as fair – the more effort and contributions an employee makes relative to others, the more money they earn

Too often, incentive schemes do not meet these criteria and become a reward expected by employees. This means that when a scheme is altered or a payment isn't made, employees can see it as unfair and inequitable, and employee satisfaction and motivation decrease.

Focus on the achievement of specific goals

Consider the goal setting process outlined within the 'managing performance' section of Chapter 4. The same principles of commitment, clarity, challenge, complexity and feedback need to be considered when you're setting goals for an incentive scheme, the difference being that the goals are more likely to be quantifiable and are often referred to as KPIs. Where individual KPIs are tied to the company KPIs, perceptions of equity may be easier to maintain.

The example in Chapter 4 is of Isaac, the events coordinator, and the company goal to have an NPS of sixty-two or higher. Isaac's personal goal is to develop a step-by-step process for a new product launch event. If the company is providing an incentive scheme to Isaac, then KPIs for his role may be that the new product achieves X number of sales. This way, the KPIs for an incentive payment are related to the goals used to measure and manage his overall performance.

I recommend having an overarching hurdle for anyone in the organisation to be eligible to receive a payment, usually related to the company's profit target being met. This way, you know the company can afford the extra payments. It also helps to create a collective mindset that the company's success is shared with the employees.

Be perceived as fair

Unfortunately, most incentive schemes I come across are expensive and largely serve to demotivate employees. This is because of common misconceptions around inequities or fairness:

- That not every employee is eligible
- A perceived secrecy around the scheme and who is eligible and why
- Non-quantifiable goals, which mean lots of manager discretion regarding who receives what level of payment
- People believing they worked hard for long hours, but were not rewarded for it in comparison with employee X
- People not receiving the same payment as last year, although they believe they worked just as hard

I could probably add more to this list. You may be wondering at this point if incentive schemes are worth the expense. The frustrating answer is that it depends on your industry, your business and your employees.

If there is an expectation for an incentive scheme in your industry, it may be difficult to attract great people – even if you are paying more as a base salary – without one. I remember one employment candidate who was in a role with a medium base salary and a large incentive. The new employer offered him the same role with a base salary that was higher than he was currently earning overall, but with no incentive. The candidate wasn't interested and asked for the higher overall salary plus an incentive scheme.

Your business will need to maintain structure and discipline around the incentive scheme rules, including role eligibility and specific KPIs. Often, organisation leaders start with the right intention, but within a few years, everyone seems to be receiving an incentive for just doing the core components of their role.

Individual employees are also motivated differently. An incentive scheme may be important to one person, but flexibility more so to another. This is why a benefits program is so important.

Benefits

Benefits programs are not just for large corporations. No matter how small your organisation is, consider benefits and collate them into one document. You may be surprised how many you already offer, but haven't before considered as benefits. Collating them into one benefits booklet creates a tangible item you can provide to potential and new employees, while helping current employees to remember what is available to them and how your organisation cares for and supports them.

You can provide many benefits for no or minimal cost. The key is to understand your employees and what they value. If you have constructed your employer brand (Chapter 3) and have structured frameworks to listen to your employees (see the beginning of this chapter), then this should be an easy program to design.

Consider these examples:

- **Flexible working** – in relation to the location, hours and days. This continues to be reported as the top benefit that employees value.[57]
- **Volunteer day** – one free leave day per year where employees can volunteer for a charitable organisation.
- **Additional superannuation** – providing more than the required amount, having a scheme where the employer pays an additional 1–2% on top of employee contributions or paying superannuation during unpaid parental leave.
- **Purchased leave** – an employee receives forty-eight weeks of pay across fifty-two weeks, so can access an additional four weeks of leave for the year.
- **Tenure-based bonus leave** – after two years of service, an employee receives two bonus days of leave until it caps at five years with an additional five days.
- **Professional development** – providing a budget and process for employee-development plans.

- **Employee assistance program** – a free confidential counselling service for employees for a wide range of personal and work-related problems.

- **Education assistance** – contributing towards the cost of a diploma or degree.

- **Social committee** – providing a budget and schedule for social events throughout the year.

- **Service awards** – recognising service every year and rewarding milestones of employment (eg one year, three years, five years).

- **Recognition program** – providing a budget and framework for recognising team members.

- **Pet friendly** – implementing 'bring your dog to work day' a few times per year.

- **Referral rewards** – when an employee refers someone for a vacant position and that person is hired, the employee receives a payment.

This list is not exhaustive. It is designed to give you some examples of how you can introduce benefits that have minimal cost and administration but can be effective in retaining employees. Once you have collated them together into a benefits booklet, highlight a benefit in each monthly meeting or staff newsletter. This helps to market your benefits to your employees so that they keep their value as a retention tool.

Summary

To be able to keep great people, you need to have a framework for listening so that you can recognise any changes to culture before dysfunction and even toxicity creep in. Although you don't run a large corporation, you can still provide the framework to enable employees to feel that they have a career path, which is a key retention tool. Finally, recognise great performance and behaviours and reward employees for increases in productivity and the success of the business.

You've made it! You completed the Find, Grow, Keep methodology. Next, it is time to maintain all this great work you have done by measuring progress and keeping the momentum.

PART THREE
MAINTAINING A GREAT PLACE TO WORK

You've decided to go all in and build a great place to work. You have the HR frameworks in place and your people are engaged, but workplace culture isn't fixed. It continually changes.

Maintaining the great work you have done is now key so that you can monitor the success of your HR programs and build momentum. This means having the measures of success, accountability and feedback loops to maintain a great place to work well into the future.

6
Measuring

'What gets measured gets managed' – this is a saying which has been around for a while. If we don't have measurements related to our workplace culture, how do we know if we are getting results? How do we course correct quickly if things start to deteriorate? If we are seeing great results, why not make sure we are communicating that to our current and potential employees to further cement the belief that we have a great place to work?

Measures of success

If we are being intentional with our culture, we want to be able to measure the success of our programs and make sure we are getting results. Although most of us understand why measuring success and implementing KPIs is important, a study by Google and MIT Sloan showed that many company leaders don't review their KPIs or use the information to help to improve their businesses.[58] The study found that the best way to improve operational efficiency included using KPIs not just to check progress to short-term goals, but to plan strategies into the future. It is important to consider both as the aim when choosing our HR-related KPIs.

If your company goal is to create a great place to work, some related KPIs could be:

- Employee turnover
- Resignations within six months and twelve months of employment
- Absenteeism
- Talent matrices
- Engagement survey results

Employee turnover

Chapter 2 covers how to calculate employee turnover, and this is an easy metric to measure and monitor. Some organisations will break the turnover down further into employee- or employer-initiated (eg performance terminations or redundancies) or even 'regretted' and 'non-regretted' (the non-regretted are departing employees who you wouldn't rehire).

Whatever you choose, it is still important to understand the total turnover number as this will impact on the perceptions and engagement of your existing team members. If it is a high number, it may also help you to understand why some objectives or projects aren't being met.

If you do break the turnover number down, be careful not to dismiss entirely the employer-initiated or non-regretted terminations. There are still lessons to be learned from that turnover. For example, how was the person hired initially? Are there gaps in the recruitment process? How did their behaviour or performance reduce over time? Are you leading and supporting your employees as you should be?

Determine your actual turnover for the last calendar or financial year, and then track it every quarter. Report your findings at management team meetings and discuss them as you would financial data.

Resignations within six months and twelve months

Although related to turnover, this is a particularly useful metric if you have a relatively large number of employees or if this is an issue within your business. When resignations are high at these points, it means that you need to review the recruitment, onboarding and management practices.

When you receive a resignation in these early stages of an employee's time with your business, it is important to encourage the employee to provide feedback on their reasons for leaving. Within the 'Listening' section of Chapter 5 are the tools to implement to get the information you need to curb resignations at these pivotal points.

Absenteeism

If highly engaged employees are less likely to take leave, it stands to reason that high levels of absenteeism (including sick or carer's leave) in the business can be an indicator of low levels of engagement. Although the average amount of absenteeism can differ across industries, in 2019, it was reported to be an overall average of 11.2 days per employee per year.[59] This included workers' compensation, personal leave and unauthorised leave.

If this is a metric you can easily report on, then doing this monthly and monitoring the trend may be more valuable than comparing your business to the overall Australian or industry average as a lag indicator of engagement. Sometimes, reporting this metric can also uncover unexpected information.

One business I worked with many years ago had a payroll system which allowed this metric to be reported. I was stunned to discover that across a three-year period, employees had taken fewer than two days per person per year of personal (sick and carer's) leave. I advised the owner that the explanation could be:

- They had the most engaged and healthy employees anyone had ever seen, or
- Employees were working flat out and felt unable to take leave, or
- Employees weren't recording their personal leave into the self-service system and managers weren't following up once someone returned from personal leave.

As you may have already guessed, it was the third point.

Talent matrices

Within the 'growth and development' section of Chapter 4 is the talent matrix process. If you're conducting this yearly and reviewing it quarterly, it can be a good metric to monitor the number of employees over time within each of the nine squares. This gives useful information to review to assess the stages of development of your employees with moderate potential, and ensure that those with high potential have development plans and those with low performance and potential have a performance improvement plan in place.

The distribution of employees across the nine squares can also be important to monitor. For example, a client had around fifteen employees and the vast majority were considered to be low to moderate potential and meets/exceeds expectations in terms of performance. Given the size of the organisation, the owner was comfortable with that spread; more than a couple of employees with high potential created high turnover numbers as the business wasn't large enough to create long-term career paths.

Engagement survey results

You need to compare the results by category of your engagement and satisfaction survey yearly, but it is also important to decide on individual engagement questions that you will aim to improve the score on each year. For example, your metrics could be:

- Engagement survey results increase from 8/12 to 10/12 categories scoring 70% or higher

- Employees agreeing with the engagement survey question *'Overall I am extremely satisfied with my organisation as a place to work'* increase from 62% to 70%

- Employees agreeing with the engagement survey question *'I am excited about going to work'* increase from 46% to benchmark 65% or higher

The benefit of identifying key engagement survey questions to increase in score and not just the overall categories is that it focuses the management team on the core idea of increasing engagement rather than areas of job satisfaction. It also means that if you change some of the categories or questions within the categories over the years, you will still have the key questions to do a straight comparison to.

I had a client who, after many years, made the decision to move away from one survey provider to another. The ability to keep some level of comparison was a key consideration before they made the change. Although it was more difficult to do direct comparisons of scores during the first year of the new survey, there were questions that hadn't changed. Importantly, as the survey scores had been consistently above average for a few years before the client made the change, it wasn't seen by the employees as an attempt to hide poor results by changing providers.

When you're choosing KPIs, consider how easy it will be to get the data. If you only have manual systems, then resignations within six and twelve months of employment could be a difficult measure to monitor. Additionally, the results need to be meaningful to your business. If you run an organisation with traditionally low levels of absenteeism, monitoring this data over time may not provide much in terms of insights.

Accountability

Accountability is a word we often see listed in company values and it is easy to see why. Most people want to work in an organisation where each person is not just responsible for their area of work, but answerable to it, where they 'own' their areas and don't blame others.

CASE STUDY: LEAD BY EXAMPLE

I have worked with many business owners/leaders who strive to embed a culture of accountability. When this fails, it generally comes down to the leaders not having a process and consistency following it.

For example, many businesses struggle to have performance reviews completed by everyone correctly and on time. Technology is seen as the answer where the platform forces emails and forms on to employees at certain intervals with numerous reminders, but still the problem remains.

Invariably, if I speak to the owner/CEO, that top leader is not using the performance review process. They may be having conversations with their senior leaders, but they aren't following the standard that everyone else is being expected to follow. This flows down to senior leaders who then don't value the process or apply it consistently, which flows to the next level, and so forth.

MEASURING

Finally, the owner finds that they have an organisation which consistently struggles to measure and reward performance.

If you are going to commit to having a great workplace culture, then you need to not only measure success, but be accountable for the results. Where there is no accountability, the measures become meaningless numbers in a report and your great workplace culture won't sustain.

HR activity calendar

The place to start is to list the HR activities that need to occur to build your workplace culture – I've described many in this book. Add these into a simple calendar, noting the activities that will take place each month and those that will occur in different months of the year. Then assign this calendar to *one person* to be responsible for those monthly activities being completed. Ideally, this person will schedule the activities into their own calendar and include progress in them as an agenda item at regular management meetings.

For example, if your business has twenty staff and no internal HR, you may assign this calendar to the office manager, who reports directly to you as the owner. That person is responsible for coordinating the HR activities and completing them each month; they become part of the office manager's goals within the performance review process, which tie to the company goal of creating a great place to work, which has KPIs of employee turnover percentage and engagement survey results.

For example:

- Office manager goal: coordinate and complete HR activities each month
- Company goal: build a great place to work
- Company KPI: employee turnover X%; engagement survey Y%

As the owner, you are still accountable for the company goal and KPI, but the office manager is responsible and accountable for the activities that help achieve this.

Here's an example of a simple calendar:

EXAMPLE: SIMPLE CALENDAR

Each month

- Check in with new starters – organise coffee chats and monitor probation review due dates
- Send first-impression surveys and exit surveys
- New starters training on workplace behaviour (update records of existing staff completing this)

January

- Quarterly performance review
- Check policies due for review this year (two-year cycle)

February

- Yearly engagement survey Talent matrix – quarterly check
- Begin annualised salary wage reconciliations for award-covered employees

March

- Check social activity done this quarter
- Quarterly all-staff meeting

April

- Recognition program – check usage
- Employee round tables
- Quarterly performance review

May

- Yearly talent matrix process

June

- Check social activity done this quarter
- Quarterly all-staff meeting

July

- Recognition program budget check
- Check fair work award increases
- Quarterly performance review – start/end year

August

- Talent matrix – quarterly check

September

- Check social activity done this quarter
- Quarterly all-staff meeting

October

- Employee round tables
- Quarterly performance review

November

- Recognition program budget check
- WHS inspection
- Talent matrix – quarterly check

December

- Check social activity done this quarter
- Quarterly all-staff meeting

RASCI

When you have a larger business, you may also use a RASCI framework to embed the consistency and process needed to make these activities happen.[60] This is a matrix that is used to identify all the roles and responsibilities.

RASCI is the acronym for the components of the matrix:

- **R**esponsible – the person who will do the activity, there is only one R
- **A**ccountable – the person who makes the final decision
- **S**upport – the person(s) who provide support to get the activity done
- **C**onsult – the person(s) consulted before decisions are made
- **I**nform – the person who is informed after action is taken or decisions are made

For example, when it comes to the recognition program and having a yearly budget for this:

- R is the office manager
- A is the owner who provides the approval and decision around the budget
- S is the administration assistant who purchases the recognition items
- C are the management team members who are consulted regarding the proposed budget
- I are the employees who are informed of the recognition items available this year and the process they can use to recognise their team members

Summary

Choose the measures of success that are most relevant for your business and monitor and communicate the results of these KPIs. Just as vital is accountability. If there is no assignment of responsibilities and accountability for your ongoing HR activities, then they will over time stop occurring.

These two steps will help you to monitor and maintain your business as a great place to work, so that you can build momentum into the future.

7
Momentum

Culture isn't fixed, and new HR practices and employee engagement tools are continually available. To keep momentum with your great workplace, you need not just to listen to your employees, but to provide feedback loops where you are communicating back to them what you are hearing and doing with the information.

Having a focus on the future and systematically reviewing your HR practices to a one- to three-year cycle will help you to create momentum. Not only will you build a great workplace culture, you may also choose to enter employment awards to become known as the best place to work.

Feedback loops

There is a great story about behaviour that refers to a fictitious experiment. Five monkeys are in a cage with a ladder and at the top of the ladder is a bunch of bananas. Each time a monkey goes up the ladder to get a banana, it is squirted with water (which monkeys do not like at all). Soon all the monkeys learn not to go up the ladder.

The researcher then removes one monkey and replaces it with a brand-new monkey. This new monkey immediately goes up the ladder, but the other four drag it back down and punish it for trying. The new monkey doesn't know about the water and that the others are trying to protect it, just that it will be punished if it keeps trying.

Eventually, the researcher removes all the original monkeys one by one and replaces them with new monkeys. The same behaviour repeats until at the end, all five are monkeys who have never been up the ladder, yet none of them even tries because they know it is 'bad'.

My own research suggests that this experiment probably never took place, but the story continues to resonate because I have seen this happen in the workplace, and you may well have seen it too. Culture is made up of a set of behaviours, actions, inactions, shared beliefs and values. If we all believe we will be punished for climbing that ladder, it becomes our culture.

Prevention is better than cure. If you have continuing feedback loops, you can keep an eye on changes to your culture. In the 'Listening' section of Chapter 5, there are a few options to hear from your employees, and if you want to continue momentum with your culture, you need a process not just to listen, but also to feedback the information you've gained. If people don't feel they are listened to, they will stop communicating.

Consider the different listening processes you have, and then add into your communication plan milestones for feeding back the information you gain from them. For example, with engagement and satisfaction surveys, you may feedback the results at the completion of the survey, then each quarter you communicate how you are tracking to completion of the action plan.

With first-impression surveys, it will depend on the size of your organisation how you feedback that information (if you only have one new employee per quarter, it could be awkward for them). It may be that each year when giving the engagement survey results, you provide some insight to the team on how the themes match, or don't, the themes you received over the last year from the first-impression and exit surveys. If you're holding round tables every second month, then every six months, you may communicate at a team meeting the value you've received from the discussions and the collated themes.

Not only do feedback loops give you the ability to keep a pulse on the culture, but they also strengthen parts of your culture with employees who will see that you value transparency, communication and giving them a voice. If you aren't providing feedback and acting on the information gained around your culture, it can cause disgruntlement as employees wonder, 'What's the point?' As new employees join, they will then pass these sentiments on. This becomes the metaphorical ladder in the cage.

Future focused

Culture evolves; it changes and is not fixed. I have heard so many times business owners or leaders say, 'We always had a great culture, I don't know what happened.' Culture change is usually slow and not always noticeable until there is an issue, which is why keeping momentum is so important.

Just as you would review the products and services you offer to customers regularly to ensure they are relevant, you need to do the same with what you are offering to employees. As a general guide, I recommend the review cycle shown in the table, but if you receive feedback that something isn't working in between times, then prioritise reviewing it then.

HR practice	Review
Employment policies and contracts	Every two years
Recruitment processes	Yearly
Onboarding	Every two years
Leadership charter	Every three years
Performance review process	Every two years
Recognition program	Every two years
Benefits program	Every three years

Employment policies and contracts

This means checking for legislative changes and additional policies that may be required. Are the policies being followed, and if not, why not? If policies are not being followed, that may suggest you need to make some changes.

Recruitment processes

The employment market continually evolves and recruitment is one of the biggest drivers of your culture. Who you hire in to the business can have a huge impact on team dynamics and productivity, so the effectiveness of your processes needs to be reviewed every year.

Here are some questions to ask yourself to start the review:

- Are you receiving the right kinds of candidates?
- Are new employees meeting expectations in terms of behaviours and performance?
- Are there any new tools available in the market that will help you hire more effectively?
- Are you advertising in the right channels?
- Are the people you are hiring performing?
- Are they staying?

Onboarding

Even the best-intentioned leaders can drop the ball when it comes to onboarding employees and introducing them to the organisation. First-impression surveys will help you to know how effective your onboarding is, but every two years, make a formal check to see if the processes are being followed and if they need to be improved.

Leadership charter

Like company values, your leadership charter (and team charter if you have one) shouldn't be stagnant. Over three years, a lot can happen in a business. The charter(s) may not be completely overhauled, but there may be some components that need refreshing to make sure that it remains relevant.

Performance review process

This is a process that often stops being completed or is done in a minimal and ineffective way. When it's first introduced or majorly changed (eg from yearly to quarterly), you may seek feedback and adjust the process after just a year. After that, it is a good idea to seek feedback from employees and managers every two years around if there is value in the process and how it can be further honed to meet the objectives of meaningful discussions around goals, performance and development.

Recognition program

Most recognition programs need a change after two years and a more significant change after three. Part of keeping recognition meaningful and personal is changing the types of rewards you offer and the mechanisms for providing the recognition. This keeps everyone engaged and motivated to continue with recognising others.

Benefits program

New benefits often come on to the market, so make sure you keep looking around. You may also discover that some of the benefits you already offer haven't been accessed at all and there's no value in continuing with many of them. It is important to remember that removing any benefits, even if they're not accessed, can be a large point of contention, so do so only after consideration and consultation.

I've come across several organisation leaders who reduced the value of service awards, for example. In the past, an employee may have received a pen and $500 for five years of service and now they just receive $100 and a thank you card. In reducing the value of the service reward, the leader may have reallocated the budget to other areas which benefit everyone, but the employees forget or don't realise that part. Even years later, they talk about how cheap the organisation is for cutting down the service awards.

Each time you review your programs and conduct an employee engagement and satisfaction survey, you have an opportunity to take your culture to the next level. After two to three years of building momentum, you may find it's time to enter some employment awards so your business receives external recognition and internal validation for the great things it is doing. Even if you don't win an award, the process of applying will give you valuable information about how you compare to similar-sized organisations that are doing great things. Just being shortlisted is a reason for celebrating and helps cement with your teams how important people and culture are to you and your business.

Summary

Add into your communication plan the milestones of where you will be providing a feedback loop. This will probably only be a few times a year, but it is an important step for employees to feel they are being listened to and that their feedback is important.

Also note in your HR activity calendar the one- to three-year review cycle for your HR practices. This will make sure you keep momentum with your workplace culture, and may give you the data and confidence to enter employment awards to validate externally and internally that you have a great place to work.

Conclusion

This is such an exciting time for your business. You have chosen to read this book, which is a great first step. Most of you are likely to know that building a great place to work is important; now you have the HR formula to make it happen.

The Find, Grow, Keep methodology I have shared with you has worked for organisations from 10–100 employees across different service-based industries to improve their workplace culture and increase engagement. This enables lower employee turnover and higher productivity, but what you may notice is that it also makes the workplace feel different. Often, owners will reflect after a year on the energy their business now has, how everyone seems to be moving in one direction and they are able to just get stuff done (GSD).

CASE STUDY: A PLAN FOR TRANSFORMATION

A few years ago, Jane contacted me as she had just started with a new company as finance manager and she recognised that the workplace culture wasn't quite right. The leadership team were open to doing a review, but they had been there for a long time and didn't see what Jane could with new eyes.

After conducting a compliance review and staff engagement and satisfaction survey, I discovered there were some key aspects the business needed to improve to meet not just certain obligations around policy and employment contracts, but also several areas where the employees were highly dissatisfied. After consulting with Jane and the leadership team, I created a HR action plan and implemented the new or changed HR practices. Soon, employees' energy was transformed. People were seeking me out and saying how wonderful it was that the organisation had started this journey. Managers were commenting on how much everyone appreciated that the business wanted to make these changes.

Since then, I have conducted a new staff survey every year. I am so pleased to report that not only did the results go up the second year, but they have continued to improve each year, including during the major change and disruption of 2020. What started as a feeling from a new manager, set the organisation on a path to become, and remain, a great place to work. Apart from quantifiable results within the engagement survey, Jane reports that there are fewer employee grievances and more innovations, and the organisation has the ability to hire high-quality people and adapt to change with more willingness and openness.

CONCLUSION

You now have the information within this book to do the same, but you may be wondering at this point who in your business should take ownership and build these HR practices, and how long it will take. My business Amplify HR implements this methodology, called the Find, Grow, Keep program, in twelve weeks. Just go to www.findgrowkeep.com.au for more information.

I am passionate about workplaces building great HR so that we can all create better and more successful businesses and societies. I wish you all the best on your journey and would love to hear your stories. Just get in touch via contact@amplifyhr.com.au or send me a message via LinkedIn and we can start a conversation. I am excited for what lies ahead for you as you grow your people and grow your business.

References

1 'Hays Salary Guide Australia 2021' (Hays, 2021) www.hays.com.au/salary-guide [Accessed 10 Nov 2021]
2 '2018 workplace learning report: The rise and responsibility of talent development in the new labor market' (LinkedIn Learning, 2019) https://learning.linkedin.com/content/dam/me/learning/en-us/pdfs/linkedin-learning-workplace-learning-report-2018.pdf [Accessed 10 Nov 2021]
3 'Fourth Industrial Revolution' (World Economic Forum, 2017) www.weforum.org/focus/fourth-industrial-revolution [Accessed 10 Nov 2021]
4 'The future of jobs report 2020' (World Economic Forum, October 2020) www.weforum.org/

reports/the-future-of-jobs-report-2020 [Accessed 10 Nov 2021]
5 Reeves, M, Püschel, L, 'Die Another Day: What leaders can do about the shrinking life expectancy of corporations' (BCG Global, December 2015) www.bcg.com/publications/2015/strategy-die-another-day-what-leaders-can-do-about-the-shrinking-life-expectancy-of-corporations [Accessed 10 Nov 2021]
6 'Small business counts: December 2020' (Australian Small Business and Family Enterprise Ombudsman, 2020) www.asbfeo.gov.au/sites/default/files/2021-11/ASBFEO%20Small%20Business%20Counts%20Dec%202020%20v2_0.pdf [Accessed 14 Feb 2022]
7 Great Place to Work Australia: The global authority on workplace culture, www.greatplacetowork.com.au [Accessed 10 Nov 2021]
8 Rutledge, T, *Getting engaged: The new workplace loyalty* (Toronto: Mattanie Press, 2009)
9 'State of the Global Workplace: 2021 report' (Gallup, 2021) www.gallup.com/workplace/349484/state-of-the-global-workplace.aspx [Accessed 14 Feb 2022]
10 Healey, B, 'This events company pivoted from staging music festivals to selling standing desks. Here's how they created an entirely new business overnight' (Business Insider Australia, 2021) www.businessinsider.com.au/

REFERENCES

events-company-pivot-standing-desks-2021-5 [Accessed 10 Nov 2021]
11 Support Act: The heart and hand of Australian Music, https://supportact.org.au
12 'Average weekly earnings, Australia' (Australian Bureau of Statistics, 2021) www.abs.gov.au. www.abs.gov.au/statistics/labour/earnings-and-work-hours/average-weekly-earnings-australia/latest-release [Accessed 10 Nov 2021]
13 'Turnover and Retention Research Report' (Australian HR Institute, 2018) www.ahri.com.au/media/1222/turnover-and-retention-report_final.pdf [Accessed 10 Nov 2021]
14 Fowler, S, 'Reflecting on one very, very strange year at Uber' (Blog post, February 2017) www.susanjfowler.com/blog/2017/2/19/reflecting-on-one-very-strange-year-at-uber [Accessed 10 Nov 2021]
15 Ryan, P, 'Woolworths investigated after admitting it underpaid 5,700 staff up to $300m' (ABC News, 2019) www.abc.net.au/news/2019-10-30/woolworths-underpays-5700-staff-up-to-300-million-dollars/11652656 [Accessed 10 Nov 2021]
16 Fair Work Ombudsman (Australian Government, 2019) www.fairwork.gov.au
17 Kantor, J, Streitfeld, D, 'Inside Amazon: Wrestling big ideas in a bruising workplace' (*The New York Times*, 2015) www.nytimes.com/2015/08/16/technology/inside-amazon-wrestling-big-ideas-in-a-bruising-workplace.html [Accessed 10 Nov 2021]

18 Wickman, G, *Traction: Get a grip on your business* (Eos, 2011)
19 Marlowe, CM, Schneider, SL, Nelson, CE, 'Gender and attractiveness biases in hiring decisions: Are more experienced managers less biased?' (*Journal of Applied Psychology*, 1996, 81(1), pp.11–21)
20 Madera, JM, Hebl, MR, 'Discrimination against facially stigmatized applicants in interviews: An eye-tracking and face-to-face investigation' (*Journal of Applied Psychology*, 2011, 97(2), pp.317–330)
21 Schmidt, FL, Hunter, JE, 'The validity and utility of selection methods in personnel psychology' (*Psychological Bulletin*, 124(2), pp262–274) www.researchgate.net/publication/232564809_The_Validity_and_Utility_of_Selection_Methods_in_Personnel_Psychology
22 Laurano, M, 'The True Cost of a Bad Hire' (Brandon Hall Group, 2015) https://b2b-assets.glassdoor.com/the-true-cost-of-a-bad-hire.pdf [Accessed 10 Nov 2021]
23 Lagunas, K, 'New hire onboarding as a driver of employee engagement' (Training, 2014) https://trainingmag.com/new-hire-onboarding-as-a-driver-of-employee-engagement [Accessed 10 Nov 2021]
24 Klinghoffer, D, Young, C, Haspas, D, 'Every new employee needs an onboarding "buddy"' (*Harvard Business Review*, 2019) https://hbr.org/2019/06/every-new-employee-needs-an-onboarding-buddy [Accessed 10 Nov 2021]

REFERENCES

25 Pendell, R, '6 Scary numbers for your organization's c-suite' (Gallup, 2018) www.gallup.com/workplace/244100/scary-numbers-organization-suite.aspx [Accessed 10 Nov 2021]

26 'Hays Salary Guide Australia 2021' (Hays, 2021) www.hays.com.au/salary-guide [Accessed 10 Nov 2021]

27 'LinkedIn's 2018 Workplace Learning Report' https://learning.linkedin.com/resources/workplace-learning-report-2018 [Accessed 10 Nov 2021]

28 Adkins, A, 'What millennials want from work and life' (Gallup, 2016) www.gallup.com/workplace/236477/millennials-work-life.aspx [Accessed 10 Nov 2021]

29 LinkedIn's 2021 Workplace Learning Report

30 Sinek, S, *Start with why: How great leaders inspire everyone to take action* (Portfolio/Penguin, 2009)

31 Marone, M, 'Guess what's dragging down employee engagement?' (Dale Carnegie, 2020) www.dalecarnegie.com/blog/leadership-affecting-employee-engagement [Accessed 10 Nov 2021]

32 Beck, R, Harter, J, 'Managers account for 70% of variance in employee engagement' (Gallup, 2015) https://news.gallup.com/businessjournal/182792/managers-account-variance-employee-engagement.aspx [Accessed 10 Nov 2021]

33 Roethlisberger, FJ, Dickson, WJ, *The Early Sociology of Management and Organizations:*

Volume V: Management and the worker (Google Books)

34 Dweck, CS, *Mindset: The new psychology of success* (Ballantine Books, 2007)

35 HBR Editors, 'How companies can profit from a "growth mindset"' (*Harvard Business Review*, 2014) https://hbr.org/2014/11/how-companies-can-profit-from-a-growth-mindset [Accessed 10 Nov 2021]

36 Kirton, K, Gray, L, Podcast episode 2.1 'How rules affect decision making in the workplace' (Make It Work: An inside look at the modern workplace) https://open.spotify.com/episode/5OXwlaSm5j8pBF2HOPX6d0 [Accessed 10 Nov 2021]

37 'How GE replaced a 40-year-old performance review system' (Workopolis, 2016) https://hiring.workopolis.com/article/ge-replaced-40-year-old-performance-review-system [Accessed 10 Nov 2021]

38 Morris, D, 'Death to the performance review' (WorldatWork, 2016) www.adobe.com/content/dam/acom/en/aboutadobe/pdfs/death-to-the-performance-review.pdf [Accessed 10 Nov 2021]

39 'Gap Inc: Ditching performance ratings and annual reviews', www.rebelplaybook.com/bonus-plays/ditching-performance-ratings-and-annual-reviews-gap [Accessed 10 Nov 2021]

40 Buckingham, M, Goodall, A, 'Reinventing performance management' (*Harvard Business Review*, 2015) https://hbr.org/2015/04/

REFERENCES

reinventing-performance-management [Accessed 10 Nov 2021]

41 Cunningham, L, 'In big move, Accenture will get rid of annual performance reviews and rankings' (*The Washington Post*, 2015) www.washingtonpost.com/news/on-leadership/wp/2015/07/21/in-big-move-accenture-will-get-rid-of-annual-performance-reviews-and-rankings [Accessed 10 Nov 2021]

42 Colvin, G, 'Microsoft and Dell are ditching employee performance reviews' (*Fortune*, 2015) https://fortune.com/2015/10/29/microsoft-dell-performance-reviews [Accessed 10 Nov 2021]

43 Locke, EA, Latham, GP, 'A theory of goal setting & task performance' (*The Academy of Management Review*, 16 (2) pp480–483, 1991) www.jstor.org/stable/258875

44 'What is Net Promoter?' (Net Promoter Network, 2017) www.netpromoter.com/know

45 Harter, J, Adkins, A, 'Employees want a lot more from their managers' (Gallup, 2015) www.gallup.com/workplace/236570/employees-lot-managers.aspx [Accessed 10 Nov 2021]

46 Officevibe Content Team, 'Statistics on the importance of employee feedback' (Officevibe, updated 2021) https://officevibe.com/blog/infographic-employee-feedback [Accessed 10 Nov 2021]

47 Kassin, SM, Fein, S, et al, *Social psychology: Australian and New Zealand edition* (South Melbourne, Vic Cengage Learning, 2015)

48 'Job mobility in Australia' (McCrindle, 2014) https://mccrindle.com.au/insights/blog/job-mobility-australia [Accessed 10 Nov 2021]

49 Ziglar, T, 'You don't build a business' (Ziglar Inc, 2016) www.ziglar.com/articles/dont-build-business [Accessed 10 Nov 2021]

50 'Performance: Accelerated' (OC Tanner Group white paper) www.octanner.com/content/dam/oc-tanner/documents/global-research/White_Paper_Performance_Accelerated.pdf [Accessed 10 Nov 2021]

51 Chapman, G, White, P, *The 5 Languages of Appreciation in the Workplace* (Northfield Publishing, 2012) (Appreciation at Work) www.appreciationatwork.com/5-languages-appreciation-workplace-improve-employee-engagement [Accessed 10 Nov 2021]

52 MBA Inventory (Appreciation at Work) https://shop.appreciationatwork.com/collections/mba-inventory [Accessed 10 Nov 2021]

53 Kassin, SM, Fein, S et al, *Social psychology: Australian and New Zealand edition* (South Melbourne, Vic Cengage Learning, 2015)

54 Amplify HR *'Find Grow Keep'* https://findgrowkeep.com.au

55 Canales, K, 'Apple is doing everything it can to keep employees from talking about pay equity' (Business Insider Australia, 2021) www.businessinsider.com.au/apple-blocks-workers-pay-equity-slack-channel-2021-8 [Accessed 10 Nov 2021]

REFERENCES

56 Kassin, SM, Fein, S et al, *Social psychology: Australian and New Zealand edition* (Cengage Learning, 2015)
57 'Gartner HR survey shows purpose and pay are growing priorities for Australian Employees' (Gartner, 2021) www.gartner.com/en/newsroom/press-releases/2021-09-21-gartner-hr-survey-shows-purpose-and-pay-are-growing-p [Accessed 10 Nov 2021]
58 Schrage, M, Kiron, D, 'Leading with next-generation key performance indicators' (MIT Sloan Management Review, 2018) https://sloanreview.mit.edu/projects/leading-with-next-generation-key-performance-indicators [Accessed 10 Nov 2021]
59 '2019 Absence Management & Wellbeing Survey' (Direct Health Solutions) www.dhs.net.au/news/2019-absence-management-wellbeing-survey-report [Accessed 10 Nov 2021]
60 RASCI Responsibility Matrix (Management Mania) https://managementmania.com/en/rasci-responsibility-matrix

Acknowledgements

My Find, Grow, Keep methodology is the result of thousands of interactions with employees, leaders and business owners over many years. Thank you to all those people I have worked with who have enabled me to create this methodology.

I am grateful to my team Elaine, Robyn, Emma and Rob who are a support and encouragement to me each day.

Thank you to the beta readers who reviewed this manuscript and provided me with invaluable feedback and praise: Jackie Le Roux, Phoebe Brisbane, Sandy Ferguson, Elaine Pereira, Louise Gardner and Lachy Gray.

Finally, thank you to all of the business owners who have given me the privilege of working with them and enabling them to create a great place to work.

The Author

Karen Kirton is the owner and MD of Amplify HR. She believes strongly that great HR can make your business more effective, productive and profitable. Working in HR for over twenty years, Karen regularly partners with SMEs to create great places to work.

With a business degree and a graduate diploma of psychology along with experience in HR management roles in various industries across Australia, Karen has a strong background in partnering with executives and senior leaders to help them achieve higher engagement and productivity within their teams. Her areas of specialisation include people and culture strategy development and plan implementation, leadership development and coaching. Karen prides herself on being commercially aware, pragmatic and able to help leaders achieve the self-awareness to realise their personal and business goals.

Karen has worked with small, medium and large businesses across Australia, with a focus on improving performance through people. She was a senior leader in a large organisation managing a team of over twenty HR professionals and has also managed HR functions at medium-sized organisations. Since 2016, Karen has worked as a consultant to SMEs to create and enable people strategies, develop leaders and build positive workplace cultures.

Karen is passionate about self-development, reading extensively and researching latest employment trends. You can get in touch with her via:

🌐 www.amplifyhr.com.au

in www.linkedin.com/in/karenkirton

www.ingramcontent.com/pod-product-compliance
Lightning Source LLC
Chambersburg PA
CBHW070533090426
42735CB00013B/2974